PRECEPT MINISTRIES INTERNATIONAL

PEACE
WITH GOD

The Need of Every Heart

Molly McInnis Farlow
Al Whittinghill

Foreword by Kay Arthur

PEACE WITH GOD—THE NEED OF EVERY HEART
© 2014 Precept Ministries International
Published by Precept Ministries International
P.O. Box 182218
Chattanooga, TN 37421
www.precept.org
ISBN 978-1-62119-339-5

2014—First Edition
Printed in the United States of America

CONTENTS

Foreword
By Kay Arthur

How can we, as human beings who have messed up so badly ever expect to be at total peace with a holy God?

It seems impossible, doesn't it? Unattainable! Something you could never achieve no matter how much you tried!

Peace...no matter the storm, no matter the turmoil within or the trials without? It seems like a wish, a dream that could never come true.

Yet the Son of God, Jesus Christ, who lived as a man, tempted and tried and tested in every way that we are, told us there was peace in Him (John 16:33).

That is what *Peace with God—the Need of Every Heart* is all about. As a group of us (all associated with Precept Ministries International) sat around our breakfast table a number of years ago, talking and praying about the spiritual needs of people around the world, this was one of the topics God brought to our minds. And thus this study which has been written, re-written, polished and prayed over for over ten years is finally in print.

Beginning at *the beginning* of everything but God who has no beginning, Molly Farlow and Al Whittinghill are going to take you on a journey through the whole counsel of God that will help you understand with great clarity just how you and any other person can be at peace with a holy God.

Molly and Al are dear friends, seasoned teachers whom I love and admire deeply because of their unwavering faithfulness and passion to establish people in the Word of God, the Bible. Both have served on staff at Precept Ministries International and have taught God's Word in many nations of this world.

Once you do this study you will have a perfect tool for carrying out Jesus' commission to make disciples of all the nations (Matthew 28:18-20). What peace and joy will be yours if you share it with others, for you will truly be about your Father's business—explaining how to have unending peace with God through the One who is called the Prince of Peace.

How to Use This Study

If you're interested in finding peace with God, and you'd like to learn what the Bible says about it by yourself or with a small group, and you have limited time for whatever reason, this study is for you! It's ideal for self-study when you have time or for early-morning, lunch, or evening groups, Sunday-school classes, and family devotions.

If you've decided to study in a group, there's no homework; participants complete each simple weekly lesson at the same time in class. You'll observe biblical texts, mark key words, answer key questions, and then discuss your findings to produce life-changing insights.

In a group study, you or someone else can take on the role of leading the discussion. You don't have to worry about lecturing or teaching—we've provided the biblical texts, inductive study questions (who, what, when, where, why, how), and insight boxes—everything you need to get going.

Here are some helpful points for leading:

- Open the study with prayer, thanking the Lord for His Word and for the opportunity to learn from it.

- Have someone read the text aloud while others follow along. Rotate readers from text to text or read them all yourself.

- As you read the Scripture texts aloud, read slowly, allowing time to (1) call the key words aloud together as you come to them and then (2) mark them with the symbol and/or color noted. The idea is for everyone to keep pace. If you would rather not call the key words aloud, that's OK too.

- Read the REFLECT questions but make sure students answer the inductive study questions together only from the text. It's not your job to lecture or answer the questions for them.

- Discuss together how new truths you discover can and will impact your life. Make sure everyone participates in this.

- If people have cross-references or insights from their lives, give them time to share them with the group at the end of the week's study only after you've completed the study of that week's texts.

- Ask the group how they can apply the study to their prayers and lives for the week. "What is relevant to pray and do in light of the truths we learned?"

Close your study praying these prayers and also for special needs in the group.

Introduction

How can I have peace with God?

One day we will see clearly that it is peace with God that is the great need of every heart.

The deep and driving need of men and women worldwide is to have a sense of peace and well-being. Everyone is looking for what will bring them meaning and fulfillment in their lives. People search for this in an endless number of places and try a million different things to find what they are longing for. Everyone in the world is attempting to find satisfaction in his own unique way. Do you see this happening?

Some seek ultimate meaning in family relationships, some in their reputation, and others in a successful career. Others give themselves to pleasure in a lifestyle full of "what feels good" in the moment. Many are frustrated trying to find what they think they need. They settle for a life of distractions that consume all their energies. Others attempt to dull the pain of disappointment with chemicals, drugs, and other things.

We expend so much energy on trying to "fix" what is broken around us. There are broken nations, broken families, broken marriages, broken relationships, and broken lives. It seems that everything is broken in this world plagued by self-centeredness, pride, unbelief, fear, hatred, violence, corruption, and guilt. Sadly, all of man's solutions for the problems in the world are short lived and end up being just temporary substitutes for the real need—peace with God.

There is real peace—not just an absence of war between nations which people think is peace on earth, not just a lack of conflict with others or a lack of turmoil within ourselves, but true peace. It is a peace that passes all understanding, satisfying the longing of the heart when it is known. Only a truly genuine relationship with God offers lasting peace. This is the need of every heart.

You may say, "Where can I find this peace?" Well, that is what this study is all about!

Week One—*Creator and Sovereign LORD*

How can we have peace with God? Is it possible?

To understand how we can have peace with God, we must start at the beginning of human history. We need to understand who God is and what our relationship to Him is. To do this, we need to go to God's Word, the Bible, to learn what He has to say. So we'll start in Genesis, the book of beginnings. In its first pages the Bible gives us an accurate account of how the universe and man came into being. This is God's record of the creation of all things.

Let's begin by observing everything we can about God and His account of creation.

OBSERVE

Read Genesis 1:1-5:

- Mark every reference to **God** (including pronouns) with a triangle. △

Genesis 1:1-5

1 In the beginning God created the heavens and the earth.

2 The earth was formless and void, and darkness was over the surface of the deep, and the Spirit of God was moving over the surface of the waters.

3 Then God said, "Let there be light"; and there was light.

4 God saw that the light was good; and God separated the light from the darkness.

5 God called the light day, and the darkness He called night. And there was evening and there was morning, one day.

> ## INSIGHT
>
> The English word **God** in this text translates the Hebrew word **Elohim**. **El** means *strong and mighty,* and **im** is a masculine plural ending. Here it speaks of the one supreme and true deity and is used in conjunction with God as Creator.

REFLECT

As you examine the text think about what you're observing. What do you learn from marking references to *God*? Just look at what the text says, and then record below what you learn. For example, in verse one you saw that "God created the heavens and the earth." Now list the rest.

According to the text, when did creation take place? How far back does this account take us?

Where did the heavens and earth come from?

How did God bring these things into being? What does this tell you about God?

OBSERVE

As we continue looking at the creation account, what more can we learn about God?

Read Genesis 1:6-8:

- Mark every reference to **God** with a triangle. △
- Circle (*and it was so*).

Genesis 1:6-8

6 Then God said, "Let there be an expanse in the midst of the waters, and let it separate the waters from the waters."

7 God made the expanse, and separated the waters which were below the expanse from the waters which were above the expanse; and it was so.

8 God called the expanse heaven. And there was evening and there was morning, a second day.

REFLECT

Once again, let's study the text. Asking questions of the text and letting it answer helps us focus on what it says.

What did you learn about God?

What did God create on the second day?

OBSERVE

Are you wondering why we are going through the creation account? The answer is simple. We are establishing from God's Word who He is and what our relationship to Him is. Everything He created was by design, with a purpose and a plan. Understanding this is essential for comprehending how we can have peace with God.

Now read Genesis 1:9-13:

- Mark **God** (including pronouns) with a triangle. △
- Circle the repeated phrase *and it was so*
- Underline the phrase *saw that it was good*.

Genesis 1:9-13

9 Then God said, "Let the waters below the heavens be gathered into one place, and let the dry land appear"; and it was so.

10 God called the dry land earth, and the gathering of the waters He called seas; and God saw that it was good.

11 Then God said, "Let the earth sprout vegetation, plants yielding seed, *and* fruit trees on the earth bearing fruit after their kind with seed in them"; and it was so.

12 The earth brought forth vegetation, plants yielding seed after their kind, and trees bearing fruit with seed in them, after their kind; and God saw that it was good.

13 There was evening and there was morning, a third day.

REFLECT

What did you learn about God from this passage?

What did God create on the third day?

What does the fact that God created and named imply about Him?

INSIGHT
Now here's something to think about: Who has the right to name people, places, and things? Who names a son or daughter? Who names a company? The one who creates, designs, owns, and/or rules over someone or something has the right to name.

OBSERVE

Read Genesis 1:14-19:

- Mark *God* (including pronouns) with a triangle. △
- Circle *and it was so*
- Underline the phrase <u>*saw that it was good*</u>.

Genesis 1:14-19

14 Then God said, "Let there be lights in the expanse of the heavens to separate the day from the night, and let them be for signs and for seasons and for days and years;

15 and let them be for lights in the expanse of the heavens to give light on the earth"; and it was so.

16 God made the two great lights, the greater light to govern the day, and the lesser light to govern the night; *He made* the stars also.

17 God placed them in the expanse of the heavens to give light on the earth,

18 and to govern the day and the night, and to separate the light from the darkness; and God saw that it was good.

19 There was evening and there was morning, a fourth day.

REFLECT

What did you learn from this passage about God?

What did God create on the fourth day?

What two great lights did God create?

God spoke all things into existence. Have you considered how powerful His word is?

OBSERVE

Read Genesis 1:20-23:

- Mark *God* with a triangle. △

- Underline the phrase **_saw that it was good_**.

Genesis 1:20-23

20 Then God said, "Let the waters teem with swarms of living creatures, and let birds fly above the earth in the open expanse of the heavens."

21 God created the great sea monsters and every living creature that moves, with which the waters swarmed after their kind, and every winged bird after its kind; and God saw that it was good.

22 God blessed them, saying, "Be fruitful and multiply, and fill the waters in the seas, and let birds multiply on the earth."

23 There was evening and there was morning, a fifth day.

REFLECT

What did you learn about God from this passage?

What did God create on the fifth day?

What did you learn from underlining the phrase *saw that it was good*?

How often do you pause to see the goodness of God's creation?

OBSERVE

Read Genesis 1:24-31:

- Mark **God** (including any pronouns) with a triangle. △
- Circle the phrase *and it was so*
- Underline the phrases **_saw that it was good_** and **_it was very good_**.

Genesis 1:24-31

24 Then God said, "Let the earth bring forth living creatures after their kind: cattle and creeping things and beasts of the earth after their kind"; and it was so.

25 God made the beasts of the earth after their kind, and the cattle after their kind, and everything that creeps on the ground after its kind; and God saw that it was good.

26 Then God said, "Let Us make man in Our image, according to Our likeness; and let them rule over the fish of the sea and over the birds of the sky and over the cattle and over all the earth, and over every creeping thing that creeps on the earth."

27 God created man in His own image, in the image of God He created him; male and female He created them.

28 God blessed them; and God said to them, "Be fruitful and multiply, and fill the earth, and subdue it; and rule over the fish of the sea and over the birds of the sky and over every living thing that moves on the earth."

29 Then God said, "Behold, I have given you every plant yielding seed that is on the surface of all the

earth, and every tree which has fruit yielding seed; it shall be food for you;

30 and to every beast of the earth and to every bird of the sky and to every thing that moves on the earth which has life, *I have given* every green plant for food"; and it was so.

31 God saw all that He had made, and behold, it was very good. And there was evening and there was morning, the sixth day.

REFLECT

What did you learn about God verse by verse?

What did God create on the sixth day?

According to verses 26 and 27, what is different about man? In whose image was he made?

INSIGHT

The Hebrew word translated *image* means *resemblance, likeness*. This does not refer to a physical body but to spiritual, moral, and intellectual qualities. God created man (male and female) with a spirit (Genesis 2:7), making them different from the animal kingdom that operates by instinct. The spirit God placed within man gave him a unique capacity to know, love, obey, communicate, and fellowship with the loving Creator who is Spirit.

Who did God put in authority over His creation, and what was he to do?

Look at all the verses in Genesis 1 where you marked *and it was so*. What does this phrase tell you about God?

What did you learn from marking *it was very good*? Why do you think God repeated the phrase *it was good* on the previous days of creation?

What did you learn about God's goodness, His abundant desire for our highest good?

Does knowing that we are made in God's image impact how you feel about yourself and how you deal with other people?

OBSERVE

Read Genesis 2:1-4 and mark:

- *God* and *LORD God* (including pronouns) with a triangle. △
- *seventh day* (including pronouns or synonyms) with a 7.

Genesis 2:1-4

1 Thus the heavens and the earth were completed, and all their hosts.

2 By the seventh day God completed His work which He had done, and He rested on the seventh day from all His work which He had done.

3 Then God blessed the seventh day and sanctified it, because in it He rested from all His work which God had created and made.

4 This is the account of the heavens and the earth when they were created, in the day that the LORD God made earth and heaven.

INSIGHT

In the New American Standard Bible and other translations, *LORD* (written in small capital letters) translates the Hebrew consonants יהוה. The transliteration of these consonants, YHWH, has been pronounced *Yahweh* and later *Jehovah.* This name conveys the meaning *Self-existent One.*

LORD God translates the Hebrew **YAHWEH (Jehovah) Elohim.** Together they mean *Self-existent God.*

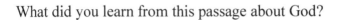

REFLECT

What did you learn from this passage about God?

Review what you learned from marking *seventh day.* How does it differ from the other six days?

According to what you have learned so far, how did the heavens and earth come into being?

Have you ever stopped to meditate upon the wonder of God's creation and the knowledge, creative wisdom, and unlimited power it took to bring everything into being from nothing? Has it ever caused you to stand in awe of Him?

From what you have observed from God's creation account in Genesis, was there harmony and peace?

Was man at peace with God, His Creator, at the very beginning?

OBSERVE

It is very important to understand and acknowledge that God, who created and sustains the heavens and the earth, is the owner and sovereign ruler over all of His creation.

There are many verses in the Bible that express God's ownership and sovereignty. Let's look at just a few of them.

Read the following Scriptures and mark:

- *God, LORD,* and *Most High* (including pronouns) with a triangle. △

Psalm 90:2

2 Before the mountains were born
Or You gave birth to the earth and the world,
Even from everlasting to everlasting, You are God.

Psalm 24:1

1 The earth is the LORD's, and all it contains,
The world, and those who dwell in it.

1 Chronicles 29:11-12

11 "Yours, O LORD, is the greatness and the power and
the glory and the victory and the majesty, indeed
everything that is in the heavens and the earth; Yours
is the dominion, O LORD, and You exalt Yourself as
head over all.
12 "Both riches and honor *come* from You, and You rule
over all, and in Your hand is power and might; and
it lies in Your hand to make great and to strengthen
everyone.

Daniel 4:34-35

34 "But at the end of that period, I, Nebuchadnezzar, raised my eyes toward heaven and my reason returned to me, and I blessed the Most High and praised and honored Him who lives forever;

For His dominion is an everlasting dominion,
And His kingdom *endures* from generation to generation.

35   "All the inhabitants of the earth are accounted as nothing,
But He does according to His will in the host of heaven
And *among* the inhabitants of earth;
And no one can ward off His hand
Or say to Him, 'What have You done?'"

INSIGHT

Nebuchadnezzar was a powerful king of Babylon, ruling from 605-562 B.C.

God Most High or ***Most High God*** translates the Hebrew name ***El Elyon.*** This name designates God as *the Sovereign Ruler over all.*

REFLECT

What did you learn about God from these passages?

INSIGHT
Sovereignty means *absolute supremacy in rule and power.* The sovereign is the ruling power: determining, administering, and having complete dominion. Although God, the Most High, grants man dominion, He alone is sovereign. Thus man was to rule under God's authority.

From these verses, what is God sovereign over?

Does your desire for control prevent you from trusting that God is sovereign? Or does it comfort you to trust that He has all things under His control?

OBSERVE

There is one more foundational truth that we need to see before we end this week's study. What was God's purpose in creating man?

Read Revelation 4:11, Acts 17:24-28, and Isaiah 43:7:

- Mark *You, Lord,* and *God* (including pronouns) with a triangle. △

Revelation 4:11

11 "Worthy are You, our Lord and our God, to receive glory and honor and power; for You created all things, and because of Your will they existed, and were created."

Acts 17:24-28

24 "The God who made the world and all things in it, since He is Lord of heaven and earth, does not dwell in temples made with hands;

25   nor is He served by human hands, as though He needed anything, since He Himself gives to all *people* life and breath and all things;

26   and He made from one *man* every nation of mankind to live on all the face of the earth, having determined *their* appointed times and the boundaries of their habitation,

27   that they would seek God, if perhaps they might grope for Him and find Him, though He is not far from each one of us;

28   for in Him we live and move and exist, as even some of your own poets have said, 'For we also are His children.'"

Isaiah 43:7

7   "Everyone who is called by My [God's] name,
And whom I have created for My glory,
Whom I have formed, even whom I have made."

REFLECT

Why did God create man?

List below any additional insights you gleaned about God.

What does God's Word, the Bible, say about God's original purpose in creating man?

INSIGHT

Did you see the word *glory*? Our LORD God is worthy to receive glory from His creation. The Hebrew verb associated with the noun *glory* means *to be heavy, to give weight or importance to, to be a visible manifestation of.*

The Greek verb for *glorify* means *to estimate highly, to value, to exalt the reputation of.* When we glorify God we magnify who He is in our thoughts, words, and actions; we esteem and praise Him. As His representatives and ambassadors on earth, we fellowship with Him and express to others truths about Him that are praiseworthy: His will, His ways, and His life.

God is good and holy (Revelation 4:8), and life and peace come only from being in a loving relationship with Him. This relationship develops increasing trust, continuing submission, and loving obedience to His revealed will.

In light of what you've learned about God, are men today fulfilling His purpose in creation and living accordingly? Why or why not?

The Heart of The Matter

As we draw our study to a close this week, it's helpful to review key principles we learned and apply them to our own lives.

This week we observed what the Bible says about the creation of the heavens and the earth. The truths we have seen are foundational for understanding how we can have peace with God:

- God is eternal, existing before time began.
- At the beginning of time God created the heavens and the earth and all that is within them.
- God owns everything He created.
- God is all-powerful. He spoke all things into existence from nothing.
- God is the Sovereign Ruler over all His creation. "…He does according to His will in the host of heaven and *among* the inhabitants of earth" (Daniel 4:35b).
- All God does is good.
- In His goodness, before God created man, He provided everything man needed for his existence and well-being.
- God created man in His own image.
- God created man to be in relationship with Himself.
- God created man to rule His creation under His authority.
- God is personal: He speaks, creates, sees, and blesses.
- In the beginning man was at peace with God.

This week we also learned that God created man to:

- glorify Him by reflecting His character and ways.
- live in a loving relationship with Him.
- bring Him pleasure.

What is the most significant insight you have learned from this week's study?

Are you living according to God's original plan and purpose?

Creation teaches us about God's power and authority, but to know Him, we also need to understand His attributes, who He is.

During the week, go back and review what you have written about God. To help you know and understand God more fully, you can reflect on His attributes that are shown in the accompanying chart.

Attributes of God	
NATURAL (Inwardly in Himself)	**MORAL** (Outwardly to His Creation)
Omniscient: Knows all	**Holy:** Morally excellent, righteous
Omnipresent: Present everywhere	**Wise & Good**
Omnipotent: All-Powerful	**Truthful:** Cannot lie
Eternal, Everlasting: Has always existed	**Loving:** Unconditional while we were still sinners
Immutable: Never changes	**Long-Suffering:** Slow to anger
Self-Sufficient: Effects His will without help	**Just:** Decides with fairness and without partiality
Self-Existent: not dependent on anyone or anything for existence	**Wrathful:** Hates all unrighteousness
Incomprehensible: Beyond man's understanding	**Merciful:** Compassionate toward those who offend Him
Infinite: Not bounded in any way	**Jealous:** Unwilling to share what is rightfully His
Transcendent: Above, apart from His creation	**Faithful:** Keeps His promises

Week Two—*God and Man Separated by Sin*

Last week we saw that God existed before time began and is the eternal, all-powerful Creator. He created the heavens, the earth, and all that is within them, including man in His own image. As Creator and Owner, God sovereignly rules over all His creation according to His will.

We also learned that God created man to glorify Himself by reflecting His character and ways. Man was created to live his life enjoying a loving relationship with God, continually seeking to know Him and bring Him pleasure.

There was harmony in all God's creation and peace between God and man from the beginning.

What happened? How did man lose his peace with God His Creator? This week we see from Genesis what happened.

OBSERVE

What did man do to destroy His peace with God?

Let's look at God's first command to man.

Read Genesis 2:15-17:

- Mark *LORD God* with a triangle. △

Genesis 2:15-17

15 Then the LORD God took the man and put him into the garden of Eden to cultivate it and keep it.

16 The LORD God commanded the man, saying, "From any tree of the garden you may eat freely;

17 but from the tree of the knowledge of good and evil
    you shall not eat, for in the day that you eat from it
    you will surely die."

REFLECT

What did you learn from marking LORD *God*?

Why did God put man in the garden of Eden?

What did God command man to do?

Because God is the sovereign ruler over all that He has created, does
He have the right to determine rules and command man? What is man's
appropriate response?

What was God's warning to man?

OBSERVE

These next verses are crucial for understanding how man lost his relationship
and peace with God.

Read Genesis 3:1-5:

- Mark **the serpent** (including the pronoun **he**) with a pitchfork.

- Circle (**the woman**) (including pronouns **you, we,** and **your**).

Genesis 3:1-5

1   Now the serpent was more crafty than any beast of the field which the LORD God had made. And he said to the woman, "Indeed, has God said, 'You shall not eat from any tree of the garden'?"

2   The woman said to the serpent, "From the fruit of the trees of the garden we may eat;

3   but from the fruit of the tree which is in the middle of the garden, God has said, 'You shall not eat from it or touch it, or you will die.'"

4   The serpent said to the woman, "You surely will not die!

5   "For God knows that in the day you eat from it your eyes will be opened, and you will be like God, knowing good and evil."

REFLECT

Look at the places you marked *serpent*. List below what the text says about him.

It is interesting to note that the woman was talking to a serpent. How did she answer him? Was she accurate in everything she said?

Compare what the serpent said against what God said in Genesis 3:1, 4 and Genesis 2:16-17.

What did you learn about the serpent's attitude toward God in this passage?

OBSERVE

Are you wondering who this serpent is? These next passages will give us insight into his identity and character. Focus on who the serpent is, not on the timing and event described. That is for a later study.

Read Revelation 12:7-9 and John 8:44:

- Mark *dragon* (including pronouns and synonyms) with a pitchfork. ⨒

Revelation 12:7-9

7 And there was war in heaven, Michael and his angels waging war with the dragon. The dragon and his angels waged war,

8 and they were not strong enough, and there was no longer a place found for them in heaven.

9 And the great dragon was thrown down, the serpent of old who is called the devil and Satan, who deceives the whole world; he was thrown down to the earth, and his angels were thrown down with him.

John 8:44

44 "You are of *your* father the devil, and you want to
     do the desires of your father. He was a murderer
     from the beginning, and does not stand in the truth
     because there is no truth in him. Whenever he
     speaks a lie, he speaks from his own *nature,* for he
     is a liar and the father of lies."

REFLECT

What do these verses tell you about the serpent?

What are his other names?

INSIGHT

The serpent's origin is found in Ezekiel 28:12-19. He, Satan, was a created being, an angel to whom God gave a special place in His presence as an anointed, "covering cherub." He was created full of wisdom, perfect in beauty, and blameless in his ways until unrighteousness was found in him. Corrupted by pride, Satan was cast out of heaven by God. Unable to touch God, Satan targeted His creation. According to Genesis 3, Satan took the form of a serpent to deceive and corrupt man, intending to thwart God's eternal purpose.

Since Satan is a liar and God's enemy, his desire is to keep us from peace with God and with others. Satan has no power against God, so he attempts to distort God's truth, discredit His character, and destroy His creation.

OBSERVE

Now look at Genesis 3:6-7:

- Circle every reference to *the woman* (including pronouns).

Genesis 3:6-7

6 When the woman saw that the tree was good for food, and that it was a delight to the eyes, and that the tree was desirable to make *one* wise, she took from its fruit and ate; and she gave also to her husband with her, and he ate.

7 Then the eyes of both of them were opened, and they knew that they were naked; and they sewed fig leaves together and made themselves loin coverings.

REFLECT

What happened when the woman believed Satan, the liar and murderer? What did she see and do?

Did the man disobey God? How?

What was the name of the tree they ate from? (See Genesis 2:17.)

What did Adam and Eve realize in verse seven? How did they respond to this knowledge?

Stop and think for a moment about what happened. When God created man, it was very good. God gave him a free will to choose to obey Him or to disobey Him, to do what was right or to do what was wrong. Man exercised his free will when he rebelled against God's clear command, moving from dependence upon and peace with God to independence, alienation, enmity, and the knowledge of evil. Everything had changed.

OBSERVE

What did God call man's disobedience?

Read the following verses in James and Romans to see how God describes it:

James 4:17

17 Therefore, to one who knows *the* right thing to do and does not do it, to him it is sin.

Romans 3:9, 23

9 What then? Are we better than they? Not at all; for we have already charged that both Jews and Greeks are all under sin;

23 for all have sinned and fall short of the glory of God,

Romans 5:12, 19a

12 Therefore, just as through one man sin entered into the world, and death through sin, and so death spread to all men, because all sinned—

19a For as through the one man's disobedience the many were made sinners,…

Romans 6:23a

23a For the wages of sin is death,…

REFLECT

What word or words are repeated in each verse?

OBSERVE

Now go back and read these verses again:

- Mark *sin, sinned,* and *sinners* with an **X**.

REFLECT

List what you learned about sin. Do these passages tell you what sin is? If so, include this in your list. Also note how sin entered the world.

All men came from Adam and Eve, the first man and woman. Everyone can trace his or her ancestry back to them. How did Adam's disobedience affect mankind (Adam's descendants)?

How serious is sin? What are its consequences?

BACKGROUND

God calls what man did "sin." What is sin? What did man do?

Man believed the serpent's lie: "...you will be like God" (Genesis 3:5b). He chose to come out from under God's rightful authority and rule. Man determined to rule his own life on his own terms.

- Sin is disobeying God.
- Sin is transgressing God's law.
- Sin is falling short of the glory of God.
- Sin is knowing what is right to do, but not doing it.
- Sin is missing the mark.
- Sin is not impersonal; it affects many.
- Sin is more than breaking rules; it is an inner independence from God.

- Sin is the attitude that God will not be God in my life and reign over me.

- Sin is living *my* life *my* way under *my* terms without regard to God, His authority, and His will.

Open or secret rebellion is repugnant to a holy God. He cannot ignore sin— He punishes sin with death, which is separation from His gracious presence.

OBSERVE

What happened after the man and the woman ate the forbidden fruit in the garden of Eden?

Read Genesis 3:8-13 to find the answer. As you read mark:

- *man* (including pronouns) with a rectangle.

- *the woman* (including pronouns and synonyms) with a circle.

- *Lord God* (including pronouns) with a triangle. △

Genesis 3:8-13

8 They heard the sound of the Lord God walking in the garden in the cool of the day, and the man and his wife hid themselves from the presence of the Lord God among the trees of the garden.

9 Then the Lord God called to the man, and said to him, "Where are you?"

10 He said, "I heard the sound of You in the garden, and I was afraid because I was naked; so I hid myself."

11 And He said, "Who told you that you were naked? Have you eaten from the tree of which I commanded you not to eat?"

12 The man said, "The woman whom You gave *to be* with me, she gave me from the tree, and I ate."

13 Then the LORD God said to the woman, "What is this
you have done?" And the woman said, "The serpent
deceived me, and I ate."

REFLECT

List what you learned from marking *man* and *woman,* including why they
hid.

What questions did God ask them? How did they respond?

Since God knows all things, why did He ask these questions?

What happened that caused man to lose his peace with God?

OBSERVE

When sin entered the world through Adam and death through sin, death then
spread to all men because all sinned (Romans 5:12). Sin has affected our
entire being: emotional, physical, and spiritual.

Now let's observe how Adam's sin spread. This is a long passage so do not
get bogged down; just look for the effects of Adam's sin.

Read Genesis 4:1-16:

- Mark *Cain* (including all pronouns and synonyms) with a **C**.

Genesis 4:1-16

1   Now the man [Adam] had relations with his wife Eve, and she conceived and gave birth to Cain, and she said, "I have gotten a manchild with *the help of* the LORD."

2   Again, she gave birth to his brother Abel. And Abel was a keeper of flocks, but Cain was a tiller of the ground.

3   So it came about in the course of time that Cain brought an offering to the LORD of the fruit of the ground.

4   Abel, on his part also brought of the firstlings of his flock and of their fat portions. And the LORD had regard for Abel and for his offering;

5   but for Cain and for his offering He had no regard. So Cain became very angry and his countenance fell.

6   Then the LORD said to Cain, "Why are you angry? And why has your countenance fallen?

7   "If you do well, will not *your countenance* be lifted up? And if you do not do well, sin is crouching at the door; and its desire is for you, but you must master it."

8   Cain told Abel his brother. And it came about when they were in the field, that Cain rose up against Abel his brother and killed him.

9   Then the LORD said to Cain, "Where is Abel your brother?" And he said, "I do not know. Am I my brother's keeper?"

10   He said, "What have you done? The voice of your brother's blood is crying to Me from the ground.

11   "Now you are cursed from the ground, which has opened its mouth to receive your brother's blood from your hand.

12   "When you cultivate the ground, it will no longer yield its strength to you; you will be a vagrant and a wanderer on the earth."

13   Cain said to the LORD, "My punishment is too great to bear!

14   "Behold, You have driven me this day from the face of the ground; and from Your face I will be hidden, and I will be a vagrant and a wanderer on the earth, and whoever finds me will kill me."

15   So the LORD said to him, "Therefore whoever kills Cain, vengeance will be taken on him sevenfold." And the LORD appointed a sign for Cain, so that no one finding him would slay him.

16   Then Cain went out from the presence of the LORD, and settled in the land of Nod, east of Eden.

REFLECT

What did you learn about Cain?

Was Cain at peace with God? Was he concerned about his sin or only about his punishment?

How did Cain's loss of acceptance or peace with God affect his relationship with his brother?

BACKGROUND

Sacrifices and offerings were the means of approaching God. Cain did not offer a sacrifice the way the LORD required, so his sacrifice was not accepted. He did not come by faith according to the word of the LORD. God had made it clear that it was by a blood sacrifice that sins would be forgiven. Cain rejected this and presented the fruit of his hard work. By faith Abel offered a blood sacrifice in accordance with the LORD's command and his sacrifice was accepted.

We must come to the LORD His way. We cannot come to Him our way, with our terms, and be acceptable to Him.

The Heart of The Matter

This week we observed the biblical account of the fall of man from God's original plan and purpose. Take a few minutes and review what you have learned from your observations.

When man ate the forbidden fruit his wife gave him, he disobeyed God's clear command. This willful disobedience caused sin to enter the world and death through sin. It brought condemnation to all men. By disobeying God man not only sinned, he also became a sinner.

God called out to the man after he sinned. Adam and his wife hid from God for the first time. Their sin had separated them from Him. God took the initiative, confronting the man and the woman, desiring them to take responsibility for their sin. Instead, they each blamed someone else.

Now consider your own situation. When you do something wrong, do you try to hide it? Do you blame others? What should you do instead?

Sin is now universal because Adam and Eve are the ancestors of all humanity. All men and women have come under the devastating effects of sin. We saw this vividly illustrated in Cain. Some manifestations of sin are lying, disobedience, stealing, cheating, anger, violence, impurity, immorality, sensuality, idolatry, greed, covetousness, envying, drunkenness, and boasting (1 Corinthians 6:9-10, Ephesians 5:3-5, and Galatians 5:19-21).

A holy God cannot ignore sin. It must be judged and punished. Instead of being at peace with God, man is now under the judgment and wrath of God. Without divine intervention, man faces eternal death—separation from God's love and goodness forever. Therefore every man is in desperate need of a Savior.

Are you living your life God's way or your way? Give this some thought.

Do you have peace with God? If not, do you have a desire for it?

Week Three—*God's Promise to Send a Deliverer*

Last week we learned that man willfully rebelled against the LORD God, his Creator. Man chose to disobey God, desiring to become a god to himself rather than submitting to his Creator. Instead of being God-centered and God-ruled, he was now self-centered, ruling his own life based on the dictates of his own self-interests and self-centeredness. Thus he failed to heed God's warning and was punished by God with separation from Him, resulting in death and its consequential anxiety. Rather than being at peace with God, man had now become His enemy, unable to free himself from the grip and power of sin.

OBSERVE

Did God abandon man in his sin to suffer the consequences of his rebellion, or did He plan a way to be restored?

Today we will look at God's plan and promise to send a Deliverer to bring man back into a right relationship with Him.

Read Genesis 3:14-15 and mark:

- *LORD God* (including pronouns) with a triangle. $\triangle$
- *the serpent* (including pronouns) with a pitchfork. ψ

Genesis 3:14-15

14 The LORD God said to the serpent,
       "Because you have done this,
         Cursed are you more than all cattle,
         And more than every beast of the field;
         On your belly you will go,
         And dust you will eat
         All the days of your life;

15   And I will put enmity
Between you and the woman,
And between your seed and her seed;
He shall bruise you on the head,
And you shall bruise him on the heel."

REFLECT

What did you learn about God's judgment of the serpent?

BACKGROUND

Genesis 3:15 is an amazing prophecy of God's eternal plan. The LORD tells the serpent He is going to put enmity (hostility) between him (the serpent, the devil) and the woman and between the serpent's seed (offspring, descendant) and the woman's seed. You can see that the woman's seed is a "he." [Note: seed is a synonym for offspring, descendant.]

What follows is a record of the first promise of the Savior or Deliverer. He will be a descendant of the woman and will bruise (***crush*** according to the Hebrew term) the serpent's head (a death blow). The serpent will only bruise (crush) His heel. It is significant for us to note that in crucifixion the heel of the victim is bruised.

As we continue to study, we are going to see that God will send this Promised One to deliver man from the guilt, power, and penalty of sin. He will utterly defeat the devil and provide the way to restore man to a right relationship with Himself.

OBSERVE

Read Genesis 3:16-19, marking every reference to:

- (*the woman*)(including pronouns and synonyms) with a circle.

- |*Adam*|(including pronouns and synonyms) with a rectangle.

Genesis 3:16-19

16 To the woman He said,
      "I will greatly multiply
      Your pain in childbirth,
      In pain you will bring forth children;
      Yet your desire will be for your husband,
      And he will rule over you."

17 Then to Adam He said, "Because you have listened to the voice of your wife, and have eaten from the tree about which I commanded you, saying, 'You shall not eat from it';
      Cursed is the ground because of you;
      In toil you will eat of it
      All the days of your life.

18   "Both thorns and thistles it shall grow for you;
      And you will eat the plants of the field;

19   By the sweat of your face
      You will eat bread,
      Till you return to the ground,
      Because from it you were taken;
      For you are dust,
      And to dust you shall return."

REFLECT

What did you learn from marking *the woman*?

What did you learn from marking *Adam*?

Why were the man and the woman punished?

OBSERVE

Read Genesis 3:20-24 and mark:

- *LORD God* (including pronouns) with a triangle. △
- *Eve* and *wife* (including pronouns) with a circle. ◯
- *Adam* and *the man* (including pronouns) with a rectangle. ▭

Genesis 3:20-24

20 Now the man called his wife's name Eve, because she was the mother of all *the* living.

21 The LORD God made garments of skin for Adam and his wife, and clothed them.

22 Then the LORD God said, "Behold, the man has become like one of Us, knowing good and evil; and now, he might stretch out his hand, and take also from the tree of life, and eat, and live forever"—

23 therefore the LORD God sent him out from the garden of Eden, to cultivate the ground from which he was taken.

24 So He drove the man out; and at the east of the garden of Eden He stationed the cherubim [guarding angelic beings] and the flaming sword which turned every direction to guard the way to the tree of life.

REFLECT

What did you learn from marking *Eve*?

What did you learn from marking *Adam*?

According to these verses, what did God provide?

From what did God make garments to clothe Adam and Eve?

What can we reasonably conclude about what happened to the animal?

BACKGROUND

Last week we read about man's feeble and inadequate attempt to cover his shame and guilt by sewing together fig leaves. Genesis 3:21 speaks of God's making garments of skin to clothe them. An innocent animal's blood had to be shed for their sin. This was the first time blood was shed on earth, the first substitutionary sacrifice. Leviticus 17:11 says, "'For the life of the flesh is in the blood…; it is the blood by reason of the life [that it represents] that makes atonement.'" The Hebrew word for **atonement** means *cover, expiation.* Here the LORD God is making an acceptable but temporary covering for Adam and Eve's sin until the Promised One comes who will crush the head of the serpent, ensuring his total destruction.

The LORD God then banished them from the garden of Eden where they had enjoyed the blessings and unbroken fellowship of the presence of the LORD. As we continue to read God's Word, we learn that God will send this Promised One to deliver man from his sin and its consequences and to restore mankind to a right relationship with Himself.

Now we will trace with broad strokes God's plan to carry out His promise to redeem man from sin and its penalty—eternal death, which is eternal separation from God's love and goodness. To **redeem** means *to purchase something,* often referring to a slave in the Old Testament. The Promised One in Genesis 3:15 will redeem man out of his slavery to sin.

In Genesis 4:1-2 we read that Adam and his wife had children. The generations that followed them were characterized by sin and rebellion against God with few notable exceptions. At one point, when man's wickedness became exceedingly great, God judged the world by sending a universal flood to kill everyone on the earth except Noah and his family. God did this not only to punish the wickedness of man, but also to preserve a righteous lineage through which the Promised One would come. Noah was one of the notable exceptions; he found grace (favor) in the sight of the LORD. He was righteous, blameless, and walked with God (Genesis 6:9b).

The generations after Noah also rebelled against God, and He judged them by confusing their common language and scattering them across the face of the earth according to their multiple languages (Genesis 11:8-9). This forced man to abandon his unified rebellion against God at Babel (Genesis 11:1-7).

After this, God called a man named Abram (later renamed Abraham). Through this man, God planned to bring the Promised Deliverer introduced in Genesis 3:15. This Promised Deliverer is God's only way to bring man back to Himself and man's only hope that he might have peace with God.

OBSERVE

Now let's trace the genealogy of the Promised One beginning with Abram.

Read Genesis 12:1-3, 7 and mark:

- *Lord* (including pronouns) with a triangle. $\triangle$
- *bless, blessing,* and *blessed* with a cloud. $\mathbb{C}\mathbb{C}\mathbb{C}$

Genesis 12:1-3, 7

1 Now the L<small>ORD</small> said to Abram,
  "Go forth from your country,
    And from your relatives
    And from your father's house,
    To the land which I will show you;
2   And I will make you a great nation,
    And I will bless you,
    And make your name great;
    And so you shall be a blessing;
3   And I will bless those who bless you,
    And the one who curses you I will curse.
    And in you all the families of the earth will be
      blessed."

7 The L<small>ORD</small> appeared to Abram and said, "To your descendants I will give this land." So he built an altar there to the L<small>ORD</small> who had appeared to him.

REFLECT

What did you learn from marking *Lord*?

What did you learn from marking *blessing*?

What else did the LORD promise Abram in verse 7?

OBSERVE

Let's look at a New Testament verse that will give us insight into the Genesis 12 passage we just observed.

Read Galatians 3:8:

- Draw a triangle around **God.** △

- Underline *Scripture.*

Galatians 3:8

> 8 The Scripture, foreseeing that God would justify the Gentiles by faith, preached the gospel beforehand to Abraham, *saying*, "ALL THE NATIONS WILL BE BLESSED IN YOU" [Genesis 12:3].

INSIGHT
New Testament Scriptures appearing in SMALL CAPS, as in Galatians 3:8, indicate direct quotes from the Old Testament. The Scripture reference inside the brackets following the Old Testament quote gives the location of the reference.

In this Scripture we see some new words:

- *Justify*—to put someone in right standing with another. Here it means to make right with God, to declare righteous.

- *Gentiles*—refers to all the nations, peoples, and families that are not Hebrews (Jews).

- *Gospel*—means "good news" of the Promised One.

- *Faith*—to believe, to take someone at his word, to trust him, and to act on what he says.

REFLECT

According to this verse, what is God going to do and how?

What was preached to Abraham?

How were Gentiles going to be justified by God?

OBSERVE

Now go back to Genesis 12:3 and underline what Galatians 3:8 refers to.

If all the families of the earth were going to be blessed "in Abraham," then Abram and his wife Sarah would have to have a son. But they were childless.

> ## INSIGHT
>
> According to Genesis 15:1-2, the LORD God told Abram not to fear because He would be his shield, and Abram's reward would be great—a son to be his heir. Because Abram was advanced in years and had no son, his servant was his heir, which was the custom at that time.

Let's look at the LORD's promise to Abram.

Read Genesis 15:3-6, where the LORD is speaking to Abram, and mark:

- *LORD* (including pronouns) with a triangle. △
- *Abram* (including pronouns) with a box. ☐

Genesis 15:3-6

3 And Abram said, "Since You [Lord God] have given no offspring to me, one born in my house is my heir."

4 Then behold, the word of the Lord came to him, saying, "This man will not be your heir; but one who will come forth from your own body, he shall be your heir."

5 And He took him [Abram] outside and said, "Now look toward the heavens, and count the stars, if you are able to count them." And He said to him, "So shall your descendants be."

6 Then he believed in the Lord; and He reckoned it to him as righteousness.

REFLECT

What did the LORD say to Abram when he suggested that his servant become his heir?

How did Abram respond to God's promise? What was the result?

What did Abram believe about God that caused him to be "reckoned [counted] as righteous"?

OBSERVE

Let's look at a New Testament verse that comments on this passage we just observed. It will give us even more insight into Abram's belief.

INSIGHT

As you observe Galatians 3:16, note that **Christ** is the Greek word for the Hebrew word **Messiah** which means *anointed one.*

Read Galatians 3:16:

- Mark **seed** and **seeds** (including pronouns) with a circle.

Galatians 3:16

> 16 Now the promises were spoken to Abraham and to his seed. He does not say, "And to seeds," as *referring* to many, but *rather* to one, "And to your seed," that is, Christ.

REFLECT

Who is the "seed" of Galatians 3:16?

Let's stop for a minute and summarize. Abraham (Abram) is remarkable in that he trusted God to do what He promised. Advanced in age and after a lifetime of childlessness, Abraham trusted God for what seemed impossible: a son, and through this son, a Deliverer.

Let's put together what we have observed in these key verses. Abraham had the Gospel preached to him. This Gospel involved the promise of the seed, Christ, the Messiah to come, who would deliver man from his sin.

Abraham's faith, which was reckoned to him as righteousness, was believing the LORD God's Word. He believed the LORD would send the Messiah who was first promised in Genesis 3:15. This Messiah would be Abraham's seed and would come from his descendants (seeds), who would be as innumerable as the stars of the sky.

OBSERVE

The passage that follows continues the LORD's promise to Abram to give him an heir from his own body and as many descendants as the stars. But now the LORD promises him something else.

Read Genesis 15:7-8, 18 and mark:

- *LORD* (including pronouns) with a triangle. △
- *Abram* (including pronouns) with a box.
- *covenant* with a slash (symbolic of cutting). /

Genesis 15:7-8, 18

7 And He said to him [Abram], "I am the LORD who brought you out of Ur of the Chaldeans, to give you this land to possess it."
8 He said, "O Lord GOD, how may I know that I will possess it?"

18 On that day the LORD made a covenant with Abram, saying,
"To your descendants I have given this land,
From the river of Egypt as far as the great river,
the river Euphrates:"

REFLECT

What did you learn from marking *Abram*?

What did the LORD promise Abram?

How did the LORD guarantee His promise to Abram?

BACKGROUND

A *covenant* is *a solemn, binding oath between two parties,* where one is usually stronger than the other. Jeremiah 34:18-19 describes the concept of men passing between the pieces of a slain calf in making a covenant with God.

According to Genesis 15:8-18, the LORD made a covenant with Abram so that Abram would know with certainty that the LORD would keep His Word concerning the Promised One (the Messiah) and the promised land. Covenants were usually bilateral (two-sided), but this one was unilateral (one-sided)—not conditioned on Abram's obedience. When the LORD re-confirmed this covenant (Genesis 17:1-8), He changed Abram's name from "exalted father" to Abraham, "father of multitudes," saying, "I have made you the father of a multitude of nations."

Abraham had two sons, Ishmael and Isaac, both whom he loved. The LORD chose Isaac to receive the promises He gave Abraham. He confirmed these promises to Isaac with a covenant (Genesis 26:1-5).

The LORD then chose Isaac's son Jacob to receive the promises, confirming them with a covenant according to Genesis 28:1-4, 13-15.

The Heart of The Matter

This week we observed God's promise and plan to send a Deliverer to bring man back into a right relationship with Him. Let's review what we learned from what we observed:

- After God confronted Adam and his wife with their sin, He addressed the serpent, the woman, and then Adam.

- While addressing the serpent, God gave the man and woman the first promise of a Savior who would crush (utterly destroy) the head of the serpent (Genesis 3:15).

This week we saw that this Promised One, the Christ, the Deliverer, was of the seed of:

- the woman, Eve.

- Abraham.

- Isaac.

- Jacob (later renamed Israel).

We also saw that:

- The LORD God told Adam and Eve about His immediate and ongoing punishment of their sin.

- Sin is now universal because Adam and Eve are ancestors of all mankind.

- Man is now under the judgment and wrath of God.

- Without divine intervention from the Promised One, all men face eternal death.

- Man's only hope is for this Savior to come.

- Only this Savior can bring us peace with God.

Is this the cry and longing of your heart? Imagine what peace this knowledge of a promised Savior can bring you as you trust the LORD and His Word.

Abraham was called to leave the familiar and to follow God into the unknown. He trusted God. Is God calling you to trust Him in unknown territory in your search for peace with Him?

Week Four—*Prophecies of the Coming Messiah*

Last week we examined the LORD's first promise of salvation from sin—a Savior (Deliverer) who will crush (utterly destroy) the head of the serpent who lured the first man and woman to sin. With broad strokes we also began to trace God's plan to bring the Promised One into this world to reestablish a right relationship between God and man. We learned that the LORD chose Abraham, his son Isaac, and then his grandson Jacob, making a covenant with them and their descendants to guarantee this promise.

Picking up where we left off last week, we read in the book of Genesis that Jacob (Israel) had twelve sons, whose descendants became known as the children of Israel. Of these sons, God chose Judah through whom the Promised One would come. Before he died, Jacob prophesied that a descendant of Judah will rule: "The scepter [representing royal authority] shall not depart from Judah, nor the ruler's staff from between his feet, until Shiloh [referring to the Promised One] comes, and to him *shall be* the obedience of the peoples" (Genesis 49:10).

One of Jacob's younger sons, Joseph, was sold into slavery to Ishmaelite traders by his envious brothers and taken to Egypt (Genesis 37). But through God's sovereign will, Joseph was elevated to be the second highest ruler in the land, just under Pharaoh (Genesis 41). Through Joseph's high position, God then saved and united Joseph's entire family, who later joined him in Egypt during a severe seven-year famine (Genesis 41-47).

In Egypt, God multiplied the children of Israel and made them a great nation [Israel] (Genesis 46:3). The book of Exodus tells us that later a Pharaoh who did not personally know Joseph came to fear their numbers and enslaved them (Exodus 1). After four hundred years of slavery in Egypt, the LORD sent a deliverer named Moses to order Pharaoh to let His people go free. Pharaoh refused, and God sent ten plagues against Egypt and her gods

(Exodus 2–12), the last being the slaying of the firstborn. Pharaoh finally freed the Israelites but soon changed his mind and pursued them (Exodus 12-14). The LORD miraculously parted the Red Sea to enable the Israelites to escape to safety and then brought the waters back together to drown the pursuing Egyptians (Exodus 14:13-31).

After freeing His people, God gave them His Law to reveal His holiness and standard of righteousness. The books of Exodus and Leviticus teach that, as sinners, Israel was not able to come into God's holy presence, but He compassionately gave them a way to approach Him through sacrifices and offerings and the tabernacle. The books of Numbers, Deuteronomy, and Joshua explain in detail how, after forty years of wandering in the wilderness because of the children of Israel's unbelief, God raised up Joshua to lead them back into the Promised Land of Canaan.

Hundreds of years later, among Judah's descendants was David, the son of Jesse, through whom God fulfilled His promise of a royal seed (Genesis 49:10). As we continue to trace the genealogy of the Promised One, we will look at some passages about Israel's King David.

OBSERVE

Read Psalm 89:3-4 and Acts 13:22b-23 and mark:

- *LORD* and *God* (including pronouns) with a triangle. $\triangle$
- *David* (including pronouns and synonyms) with a **D.**

Psalm 89:3-4

3 "I [LORD] have made a covenant with My chosen;
   I have sworn to David My servant,
4 I will establish your seed forever
   And build up your throne to all generations."   Selah.

Acts 13:22b-23

22b "...He [God] raised up David to be their king, concerning whom He also testified and said, 'I HAVE FOUND DAVID the son of Jesse, A MAN AFTER MY HEART, who will do all My will.' [Psalm 89:20; 1 Samuel 13:14].

23 "From the descendants of this man, according to promise, God has brought to Israel a Savior..."

REFLECT

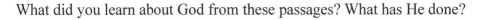

What did you learn about God from these passages? What has He done?

What did you learn about David?

According to all you've seen, who will the Promised One come from?

According to Acts 13:23, what is the Promised One called?

BACKGROUND

King David's son Solomon succeeded him (1 Kings 1). After Solomon, the nation of Israel divided into Northern (Israel) and Southern (Judah) kingdoms (1 Kings 12). For the next 200 years separate kings ruled these kingdoms until the North was taken into captivity by Assyria (722 B.C.). During this time, the Northern Kingdom disobediently worshipped false gods and their idols. Most of the time, the Southern Kingdom also mixed idolatry with their worship of God. The LORD sent prophets to call His people back to Him and to prophesy concerning the Promised One and things to come. Let's look at some of these prophecies.

OBSERVE

Read Isaiah 7:14, Isaiah 9:6-7, Daniel 7:13-14, and Isaiah 11:1-2 and mark:

- *child, son, shoot, branch,* and *Son of Man* all of which reference the *Promised One* (including pronouns and titles) with a cross. †
- *David* with a **D** (including pronouns).

Isaiah 7:14

14 "Therefore the Lord Himself will give you a sign: Behold, a virgin will be with child and bear a son, and she will call His name Immanuel."

INSIGHT
Immanuel means *God with us*.

Isaiah 9:6-7

6 For a child will be born to us, a son will be given to us;
   And the government will rest on His shoulders;
   And His name will be called Wonderful Counselor,
      Mighty God,
   Eternal Father, Prince of Peace.
7 There will be no end to the increase of *His* government
      or of peace,
   On the throne of David and over his kingdom,
   To establish it and to uphold it with justice and
      righteousness
   From then on and forevermore.
   The zeal of the LORD of hosts will accomplish this.

Daniel 7:13-14

13 "I [Daniel] kept looking in the night visions,
   And behold, with the clouds of heaven
   One like a Son of Man was coming,
   And He came up to the Ancient of Days
   And was presented before Him.
14 "And to Him was given dominion,
   Glory and a kingdom,
   That all the peoples, nations and *men of every* language
   Might serve Him.
   His dominion is an everlasting dominion
   Which will not pass away;
   And His kingdom is one
   Which will not be destroyed."

Isaiah 11:1-2

1   Then a shoot will spring from the stem of Jesse,
    And a branch from his roots will bear fruit.
2   The Spirit of the LORD will rest on Him,
    The spirit of wisdom and understanding,
    The spirit of counsel and strength,
    The spirit of knowledge and the fear of the LORD.

REFLECT

What did you learn from marking the references to the *child* and *son* in Isaiah 7 and 9?

What did you learn about the Son of Man from Daniel 7:13-14?

What more did you learn about the Promised One from Isaiah 11:1-2?

BACKGROUND

This week we continued to trace the genealogy of the Promised One through Abraham, Isaac, Jacob, Judah, Jesse, and King David. We also examined a few of the many prophecies concerning this Promised One. There are many more which we do not have time to cover. In fact, there are hundreds of prophecies in the Old Testament concerning the Promised One and His coming.

The Old Testament is also full of pictures and types that point to the Promised One. He is portrayed clearly in the sacrifices God commanded His people to offer (Leviticus 1-5). They foretell different aspects of His giving Himself for us and how He will bring us back to God through His self-sacrifice, giving us peace through His blood which He will shed on the cross.

The Messiah is also typified in every aspect of the tabernacle (Exodus 35-40). This is where God's people came to meet and worship Him. God gave Moses an exact pattern for this tabernacle, an earthly copy of the tabernacle in heaven, commanding him to build it according to His specifications because it pointed to the Messiah. This was to show His people that in order to approach a holy God one must come by substitutionary blood offered as a sacrifice for sin and with a heart of sincere repentance and faith.

OBSERVE

The Promised One is also pictured in the Passover, which we will now observe.

Read Exodus 12:3, 5-7, 11-13, and 26-27a:

- Mark *lamb* (including pronouns) with a cross. †

Exodus 12:3, 5-7, 11-13, 26-27a

3 "Speak to all the congregation of Israel, saying, 'On the tenth of this month they are each one to take a lamb for themselves, according to their fathers' households, a lamb for each household.'"

5 "'Your lamb shall be an unblemished male a year old; you may take it from the sheep or from the goats.

6 'You shall keep it until the fourteenth day of the same month, then the whole assembly of the congregation of Israel is to kill it at twilight.

7 'Moreover, they shall take some of the blood and put it on the two doorposts and on the lintel of the houses in which they eat it.'"

11 "'Now you shall eat it in this manner: *with* your loins girded, your sandals on your feet, and your staff in your hand; and you shall eat it in haste—it is the LORD's Passover.

12   'For I [the LORD] will go through the land of Egypt
on that night, and will strike down all the firstborn in
the land of Egypt, both man and beast; and against
all the gods of Egypt I will execute judgments—I
am the LORD.

13   'The blood shall be a sign for you on the houses
where you live; and when I see the blood I will pass
over you, and no plague will befall you to destroy
you when I strike the land of Egypt.'"

26   "And when your children say to you, 'What does
this rite mean to you?'

27a   you shall say, 'It is a Passover sacrifice to the LORD
who passed over the houses of the sons of Israel in
Egypt when He smote the Egyptians, but spared
our homes...'"

REFLECT

What did you learn from marking *lamb*?

OBSERVE

Read through this Exodus passage again and mark:

- *blood* (including pronouns) with three dots. ⋰

- *Passover* with a half circle. ⌒

- *LORD* (including pronouns) with a triangle. △

What did you learn about the LORD?

What did God tell His people to do with the blood and why?

Why is this called the LORD'S Passover?

INSIGHT

The Passover was, and still is, a very significant event for the descendants of Abraham, Isaac, and Jacob. The LORD ordained the Passover to picture the Promised One, the Messiah (Christ) to come.

OBSERVE

Read 1 Corinthians 5:7b and mark:

- *Passover* with a half circle.
- *Christ* with a cross. †

1 Corinthians 5:7b

7b "…Christ our Passover also has been sacrificed."

REFLECT

What did you learn from marking *Christ*?

In light of what you just studied about the Passover, what does "Christ, our Passover" mean?

INSIGHT

The Promised One's innocence is pictured in the unblemished condition of the sacrificial lambs. The Messiah will not be sacrificed for any fault of His own. His precious blood will be applied to all who believe in Him, and God will "pass over" their sins and transgressions. The Promised One's death will pay the penalty for sin once for all.

OBSERVE

The Promised One is also pictured in the Scriptures as a suffering Servant. Isaiah 53 especially shows this in graphic detail. Let's look at a few verses.

Read Isaiah 53:4-7 and 11:

- Mark **Promised One** (including pronouns beginning with **He** in verse 4) with a cross. †

- Circle *we*, *our*, *us*, and *their* (and synonyms).

> ## INSIGHT
>
> *Iniquity* in this passage means *inner crookedness, evil bent, perversity, opposition to God's law, wickedness; corrupt affections, a twisting or perversion of God's law.*
>
> *Transgress* means *to refuse to be subject to rightful authority or rebellion.* It is *willful disobedience.*

Isaiah 53:4-7, 11

4 Surely our griefs He Himself [The Promised One]
     bore,
   And our sorrows He carried;
   Yet we ourselves esteemed Him stricken,
   Smitten of God, and afflicted.
5 But He was pierced through for our transgressions,
   He was crushed for our iniquities;
   The chastening for our well-being *fell* upon Him,
   And by His scourging we are healed.
6 All of us like sheep have gone astray,
   Each of us has turned to his own way;
   But the LORD has caused the iniquity of us all
   To fall on Him.
7 He was oppressed and He was afflicted,
   Yet He did not open His mouth;
   Like a lamb that is led to slaughter,
   And like a sheep that is silent before its shearers,
   So He did not open His mouth.

11 As a result of the anguish of His soul,
   He [the LORD] will see *it and* be satisfied;
   By His knowledge the Righteous One,
   My Servant, will justify the many,
   As He [the Promised One] will bear their iniquities.

REFLECT

What did the Promised One do for you and others?

If a person does this for you, what does this tell you about His love?

According to verse 6, how are we like Adam and Eve?

What does this passage teach you about the seriousness of sin?

The Heart of The Matter

Although we swept through thousands of years of history this week, we just skimmed the surface. There are hundreds of prophecies in the Old Testament about the coming of the Promised One, the Messiah. We looked at only a few.

The Promised One, the Christ (Messiah), the Deliverer to come, will be:

- the seed of the first woman (Genesis 3:15).
- the seed of Abraham.
- the seed of Isaac.
- the seed of Jacob (Israel).
- from the tribe of Judah.
- from the stem of Jesse.
- the seed of David, King of Israel.
- the Passover lamb.
- born of a virgin.
- called "Immanuel": God with us.
- called "Wonderful Counselor, Mighty God, Eternal Father, Prince of Peace."

This Promised One will rule as King:

- with no end to the increase of His government.
- on the throne of David, which God promised to establish and uphold with justice and righteousness forever.
- with dominion, glory, and a kingdom that all may serve Him.
- with an everlasting dominion that will not pass away or be destroyed.

This Promised One, as the suffering Servant, will also:

- bear our griefs and carry our sorrows.
- be smitten by God.
- be afflicted, pierced, crushed, chastened, and scourged.
- have the iniquity of us all placed on Him.

Peace with God comes only through this Prince of Peace.

Have you come to know the Prince of Peace?

Week Five—God's Promised Messiah is Born

Last week we caught a glimpse of the genealogy and prophecies of the Promised One, the Messiah (Christ). Our goal was to establish briefly the prophesied identity and work of the Messiah.

Malachi was the last Old Testament prophet to proclaim God's Word (5th Century B.C.). After him God was silent for about 400 years until He sent John the Baptist to preach, "Repent, for the kingdom of heaven is at hand" (Matthew 3:2).

This week we will study what the Bible says about the Promised Messiah's coming to walk and live among men on earth.

Let's begin by looking at the genealogy of this Messiah. We find this in two places in the New Testament. Matthew 1:1-17 records the Messiah's genealogy from Abraham, and Luke 3:23-38 records His genealogy from Adam.

The Bible in its original languages is absolutely inerrant in everything it teaches—doctrine, ethics, and facts. Accordingly the historical context of the first Scripture we will look at this week, Matthew 1:17, is noteworthy. Abraham (through whom God promised to bless all nations) lived around 2000 B.C., and David (through whom God will raise up an eternal kingdom) around 1000 B.C. The deportation of Judah (Southern Kingdom) to Babylon under King Nebuchadnezzar occurred in three stages from approximately 605 to 586 B.C. The biblical record is corroborated by archaeology and eyewitness accounts.

OBSERVE

Read Matthew 1:1, 17:

- Mark *Jesus* and *Messiah* (including titles) with a cross. †

   Matthew 1:1, 17

   1 The record of the genealogy of Jesus the Messiah, the son of David, the son of Abraham:

   17 So all the generations from Abraham to David are fourteen generations; from David to the deportation to Babylon, fourteen generations; and from the deportation to Babylon to the Messiah, fourteen generations.

REFLECT

Whose genealogy is this?

Who are included in His genealogy?

OBSERVE

Now let's observe the angelic announcement of the birth of the Messiah.

Read Luke 1:26-35 and mark:

- *Mary* (including pronouns and synonyms) with the letter **M**.

- *son*, *Jesus,* and *Son of the Most High* (including titles, synonyms, and pronouns) with a cross. †

Luke 1:26-35

26 Now in the sixth month the angel Gabriel was sent from God to a city in Galilee called Nazareth,

27 to a virgin engaged to a man whose name was Joseph, of the descendants of David; and the virgin's name was Mary.

28 And coming in, he said to her, "Greetings, favored one! The Lord *is* with you."

29 But she was very perplexed at *this* statement, and kept pondering what kind of salutation this was.

30 The angel said to her, "Do not be afraid, Mary; for you have found favor with God.

31 "And behold, you will conceive in your womb and bear a son, and you shall name Him Jesus.

32 "He will be great and will be called the Son of the Most High; and the Lord God will give Him the throne of His father David;

33 and He will reign over the house of Jacob forever, and His kingdom will have no end."

34 Mary said to the angel, "How can this be, since I am a virgin?"

35 The angel answered and said to her, "The Holy Spirit will come upon you, and the power of the Most High will overshadow you; and for that reason the holy Child shall be called the Son of God."

REFLECT

What did you learn from marking *Mary*?

What did you learn about Mary's son from this passage?

Who will Mary's son be? What will He be called?

Since Mary was a virgin, how was it possible for her to conceive according to verse 35?

OBSERVE

Now we'll look at the birth of Jesus from the perspective of Joseph, who was engaged to Mary.

Read Matthew 1:20b-25 and mark:

- *Joseph* (including pronouns) with a **J**.

- Mary's *child* (including all names, pronouns, and synonyms) with a cross. †

Matthew 1:20b-25

20b ...behold, an angel of the Lord appeared to him in a dream, saying, "Joseph, son of David, do not be afraid to take Mary as your wife; for the Child who has been conceived in her is of the Holy Spirit.

21 "She will bear a Son; and you shall call His name Jesus, for He will save His people from their sins."

22   Now all this took place to fulfill what was spoken by the Lord through the prophet:

23   "Behold, the virgin shall be with child and shall bear a Son, and they shall call His name Immanuel," which translated means, "God with us" [Isaiah 7:14; 9:6,7].

24   And Joseph awoke from his sleep and did as the angel of the Lord commanded him, and took Mary as his wife,

25   but kept her a virgin until she gave birth to a Son; and he called His name Jesus.

REFLECT

What did you learn from marking references to Mary's *child*?

What did you learn from marking *Joseph*?

OBSERVE

This next passage gives us the angelic announcement of Christ's birth to shepherds who were tending their flocks by night near Bethlehem.

Read Luke 2:1-12 and mark:

- *Joseph* (including pronouns) with a **J**.

- Mary's *son* (include titles, pronouns, and synonyms) with a cross. †

Luke 2:1-12

1 Now in those days a decree went out from Caesar Augustus, that a census be taken of all the inhabited earth.

2 This was the first census taken while Quirinius was governor of Syria.

3 And everyone was on his way to register for the census, each to his own city.

4 Joseph also went up from Galilee, from the city of Nazareth, to Judea, to the city of David which is called Bethlehem, because he was of the house and family of David,

5 in order to register along with Mary, who was engaged to him, and was with child.

6 While they were there, the days were completed for her to give birth.

7 And she gave birth to her firstborn son; and she wrapped Him in cloths, and laid Him in a manger, because there was no room for them in the inn.

8 In the same region there were *some* shepherds staying out in the fields and keeping watch over their flock by night.

9 And an angel of the Lord suddenly stood before them, and the glory of the Lord shone around them; and they were terribly frightened.

10 But the angel said to them, "Do not be afraid; for behold, I bring you good news of great joy which will be for all the people;

11 for today in the city of David there has been born for you a Savior, who is Christ the Lord.

12 "This *will be* a sign for you: you will find a baby wrapped in cloths and lying in a manger."

REFLECT

What did you learn from marking *Joseph*?

What did you learn from marking Mary's *son*?

From reading verse 11, what did you learn about the Christ?

OBSERVE

Read Micah 5:2, a prophecy concerning the Promised Messiah:

Micah 5:2

2 "But as for you, Bethlehem Ephrathah,
   Too little to be among the clans of Judah,
   From you One will go forth for Me [God] to be ruler
      in Israel.
   His goings forth are from long ago,
   From the days of eternity."

REFLECT

How does Luke 2:4-11 relate to this prophecy in Micah?

OBSERVE

The Gospel of John takes us all the way back to the beginning and presents Christ in a unique way.

Read John 1:1-15:

- Mark **Word** and **Light** (including pronouns) with a cross. †

John 1:1-15

1 In the beginning was the Word, and the Word was with God, and the Word was God.

2 He was in the beginning with God.

3 All things came into being through Him, and apart from Him nothing came into being that has come into being.

4 In Him was life, and the life was the Light of men.

5 The Light shines in the darkness, and the darkness did not comprehend it.

6 There came a man sent from God, whose name was John.

7 He came as a witness, to testify about the Light, so that all might believe through him.

8 He was not the Light, but *he came* to testify about the Light.

9 There was the true Light which, coming into the world, enlightens every man.

10 He was in the world, and the world was made through Him, and the world did not know Him.

11 He came to His own, and those who were His own did not receive Him.

12 But as many as received Him, to them He gave the right to become children of God, *even* to those who believe in His name,

13 who were born, not of blood nor of the will of the flesh nor of the will of man, but of God.

14   And the Word became flesh, and dwelt among us, and we saw His glory, glory as of the only begotten from the Father, full of grace and truth.

15   John testified about Him and cried out, saying, "This was He of whom I said, 'He who comes after me has a higher rank than I, for He existed before me.'"

REFLECT

What did you learn from marking the references to *Word* and *Light*?

According to verse 12, what happens to those who receive the Word and believe in His name?

As stated in verse 13, what does not factor into being born of God?

OBSERVE

In the Old Testament God speaks of a chosen messenger He will send to announce the appearing of the Messiah and the beginning of His ministry. Who is this messenger?

Read Malachi 3:1a and Isaiah 40:3-5:

- Mark *messenger* and *voice* (including pronouns) with a box. ☐

Malachi 3:1a

1a "Behold, I am going to send My messenger, and he will clear the way before Me...."

Isaiah 40:3-5

3 A voice is calling,
   "Clear the way for the LORD in the wilderness;
   Make smooth in the desert a highway for our God.
4 "Let every valley be lifted up,
   And every mountain and hill be made low;
   And let the rough ground become a plain,
   And the rugged terrain a broad valley;
5 Then the glory of the LORD will be revealed,
   And all flesh will see *it* together;
   For the mouth of the LORD has spoken."

REFLECT

What will God's messenger do?

What will happen after God's messenger clears the way?

OBSERVE

The beginnings of all four Gospels give an account of this prophesied messenger. Luke 1 gives the account of his miraculous birth. Let's look at a few passages from John and Matthew.

Read John 1:19-23, 29-34 and Matthew 3:16-17 and mark:

- $\boxed{\textit{John}}$ [the Baptist] (including pronouns) with a box.

- *Jesus, Lamb of God,* and *Man* (including titles, pronouns, and synonyms) with a cross. ✝

John 1:19-23, 29-34

19   This is the testimony of John [John the Baptist], when the Jews sent to him priests and Levites from Jerusalem to ask him, "Who are you?"

20   And he confessed and did not deny, but confessed, "I am not the Christ."

21   They asked him, "What then? Are you Elijah?" And he said, "I am not." "Are you the Prophet?" And he answered, "No."

22   Then they said to him, "Who are you, so that we may give an answer to those who sent us? What do you say about yourself?"

23   He said, "I am A VOICE OF ONE CRYING IN THE WILDERNESS, 'MAKE STRAIGHT THE WAY OF THE LORD,' as Isaiah the prophet said" [Isaiah 40:3].

29   The next day he [John the Baptist] saw Jesus coming to him and said, "Behold, the Lamb of God who takes away the sin of the world!

30   "This is He on behalf of whom I said, 'After me comes a Man who has a higher rank than I, for He existed before me.'

31 "I did not recognize Him, but so that He might be manifested to Israel, I came baptizing in water."

32 John testified saying, "I have seen the Spirit descending as a dove out of heaven, and He remained upon Him.

33 "I did not recognize Him, but He [God] who sent me to baptize in water said to me, 'He upon whom you see the Spirit descending and remaining upon Him, this is the One who baptizes in the Holy Spirit.'

34 "I myself have seen, and have testified that this is the Son of God."

Matthew 3:16-17

16 After being baptized, Jesus came up immediately from the water; and behold, the heavens were opened, and he [John the Baptist] saw the Spirit of God descending as a dove *and* lighting on Him,

17 and behold, a voice out of the heavens said, "This is My [God's] beloved Son, in whom I am well-pleased."

REFLECT

What did you learn from marking *John*?

What did you learn from marking *Jesus, Lamb of God,* and *Man*?

What did God the Father say to John the Baptist concerning the identity of the Messiah?

Even though we did not have time to examine every passage concerning John the Baptist, with the verses you observed, can you see the value of comparing Scripture with Scripture to come to a fuller understanding of God's Word?

The Heart of The Matter

We learned this week that Jesus of Nazareth is the Promised Messiah (Christ). The Old Testament prophesied His coming, and the New Testament authenticated His being sent from God. He is the living Word, the Word made flesh. Scriptures prove indisputably that Jesus is the Son of God.

We saw that:

- Jesus' genealogy fulfilled the genealogy of the prophesied Messiah.
- Jesus fulfills all prophecies in the Scriptures concerning the Messiah.
- Jesus, the Word in John 1, was in the beginning with God and was God.
- "All things came into being through Him..." (John 1:3a).
- "In Him was life, and the life was the Light of men" (John 1:4).
- Jesus was the true Light, which enlightens every man (John 1:9).
- "And the Word became flesh, and dwelt among us, and we saw His glory, glory as of the only begotten from the Father, full of grace and truth" (John 1:14).
- John the Baptist, God's chosen messenger, testified that Jesus was "...the Lamb of God who takes away the sin of the world!" (John 1:29b).
- The Holy Spirit testified that Jesus was the Promised One by descending upon Jesus in the form of a dove at His baptism.
- The Father testified from heaven at Jesus' baptism that He was His beloved Son, in whom He was well-pleased.

Faithful to His promises, God's Deliverer had arrived, His identity revealed. In fulfillment of His eternal plan, thousands of years after He was prophesied, this Jesus of Nazareth, born of a virgin, came to earth to walk and live among men. Through Him we can have peace with God.

These are profound truths. What have you learned this week that has impacted your life?

Week Six—*Jesus Declares Himself to Be God*

Last week we established from the Old and New Testaments that Jesus, the virgin-born son of Mary, was the Christ. His Messianic lineage and His fulfillment of Messianic prophecies proved Jesus was, indeed, the long-awaited Promised One.

We learned that God the Father (the voice from heaven at Jesus' baptism), John the Baptist (a voice on earth), and the Holy Spirit all testified that Jesus is the Son of God.

Now let's study the Scriptures that authenticate and prove that Jesus is who He claimed to be: Jesus declared Himself to be God.

OBSERVE

In the following passage we find Jesus in Jerusalem at the pool of Bethesda. Seeing a man who had been sick for thirty-eight years, Jesus asked him if he wanted to be well. He immediately healed the man on the Sabbath. The next passage continues this account, following the man's healing.

Read John 5:14-21 and mark:

- *Jesus* and *Son* (including pronouns) with a cross. †
- *Father* and *God* (including pronouns) with a triangle. △

John 5:14-21

14　Afterward Jesus found him [the healed man] in the temple and said to him, "Behold, you have become well; do not sin anymore, so that nothing worse happens to you."

15 The man went away, and told the Jews that it was Jesus who had made him well.

16 For this reason the Jews were persecuting Jesus, because He was doing these things on the Sabbath.

17 But He answered them, "My Father is working until now, and I Myself am working."

18 For this reason therefore the Jews were seeking all the more to kill Him, because He not only was breaking the Sabbath, but also was calling God His own Father, making Himself equal with God.

19 Therefore Jesus answered and was saying to them, "Truly, truly, I say to you, the Son can do nothing of Himself, unless *it is* something He sees the Father doing; for whatever the Father does, these things the Son also does in like manner.

20 "For the Father loves the Son, and shows Him all things that He Himself is doing; and *the Father* will show Him greater works than these, so that you will marvel.

21 "For just as the Father raises the dead and gives them life, even so the Son also gives life to whom He wishes."

REFLECT

What did you learn about Jesus' relationship with His Father?

How did the Jews respond to Jesus? What did they want to do with Him? Why?

OBSERVE

Jesus repeatedly claimed to be one with God, His Father. Let's look at one of these occasions.

Read John 10:22-33 and mark:

- *Jesus* and *Christ* (including pronouns) with a cross. †

- *Father* and *God* (including pronouns) with a triangle. △

John 10:22-33

22   At that time the Feast of the Dedication took place at Jerusalem;

23b ...Jesus was walking in the temple in the portico of Solomon.

24   The Jews then gathered around Him, and were saying to Him, "How long will You keep us in suspense? If You are the Christ, tell us plainly."

25   Jesus answered them, "I told you, and you do not believe; the works that I do in My Father's name, these testify of Me.

26   "But you do not believe because you are not of My sheep.

27   "My sheep hear My voice, and I know them, and they follow Me;

28   and I give eternal life to them, and they will never perish; and no one will snatch them out of My hand.

29   "My Father, who has given *them* to Me, is greater than all; and no one is able to snatch *them* out of the Father's hand.

30   "I and the Father are one."

31   The Jews picked up stones again to stone Him.

32   Jesus answered them, "I showed you many good works from the Father; for which of them are you stoning Me?"

33   The Jews answered Him, "For a good work we do
not stone You, but for blasphemy; and because You,
being a man, make Yourself out *to be* God."

REFLECT

When the Jews asked Jesus to tell them plainly if He was the Christ, how
did He respond?

How did the Jews' reaction confirm that they understood Jesus' claim?

BACKGROUND

According to Mosaic Law, God commanded stoning (death) for sexual sins,
rebellion against authorities, kidnapping, killing, witchcraft and sorcery,
false prophecy, and blasphemy (evil, abusive, irreverent statements against
God). The harshness of the punishment shows us the seriousness of the
offense. Here the Jews accused Jesus of blasphemy saying, "...You, being a
man, make Yourself out *to be* God" (John 10:33b). Jesus' claim was worthy
of stoning if it was false. But if His claim is true, He is indisputably God in
the flesh.

Not only did the Father, the Holy Spirit, John the Baptist, and Jesus Himself
declare that He was the Son of God, but also Jesus' followers claimed the
same.

OBSERVE

In the following Scripture, note another name given to Jesus: "the Son of Man" (Daniel 7:13-14).

Read Matthew 16:13-17:

- Mark *Jesus* (including titles and pronouns) with a cross. †

Matthew 16:13-17

13 Now when Jesus came into the district of Caesarea Philippi, He was asking His disciples, "Who do people say that the Son of Man is?"

14 And they said, "Some *say* John the Baptist; and others, Elijah; but still others, Jeremiah, or one of the prophets."

15 He said to them, "But who do you say that I am?"

16 Simon Peter answered, "You are the Christ, the Son of the living God."

17 And Jesus said to him, "Blessed are you, Simon Barjona, because flesh and blood did not reveal *this* to you, but My Father who is in heaven."

REFLECT

Who did Simon Peter say Jesus was? How did he know?

What is your understanding of who Jesus is?

OBSERVE

Jesus' claim to be the Christ, the Son of the Living God, was clearly proven by His genealogy, by prophecy, by affirmation from God the Father, God the Spirit, and the prophets . . . and also by Jesus' works.

Read John 10:37-38, Acts 2:22, Mark 2:5-11, and Mark 1:39:

- Mark *Jesus* (including titles, synonyms, and pronouns) with a cross. †

John 10:37-38

37 "If I [Jesus] do not do the works of My Father, do not believe Me;
38 but if I do them, though you do not believe Me, believe the works, so that you may know and understand that the Father is in Me, and I in the Father."

Acts 2:22

22 "Men of Israel, listen to these words: Jesus the Nazarene, a man attested to you by God with miracles and wonders and signs which God performed through Him in your midst, just as you yourselves know—"

Mark 2:5-11

5 And Jesus seeing their faith said to the paralytic, "Son, your sins are forgiven."
6 But some of the scribes were sitting there and reasoning in their hearts,
7 "Why does this man speak that way? He is blaspheming; who can forgive sins but God alone?"
8 Immediately Jesus, aware in His spirit that they were reasoning that way within themselves, said to them, "Why are you reasoning about these things in your hearts?

9 "Which is easier, to say to the paralytic, 'Your sins
are forgiven'; or to say, 'Get up, and pick up your
pallet and walk'?

10 "But so that you may know that the Son of Man has
authority on earth to forgive sins"—He said to the
paralytic,

11 "I say to you, get up, pick up your pallet and go
home."

Mark 1:39

39 And He [Jesus] went into their synagogues throughout
all Galilee, preaching and casting out the demons.

REFLECT

What did you learn about Jesus in these passages?

According to John 10:37-38, Jesus said He did the works of His Father.
What does this prove?

According to Acts 2:22, who was doing the works? What did these works do?

What work was Jesus doing in the Mark 2:5-11 passage?

According to Mark 2:7, why did the Jews say Jesus was blaspheming? How did Jesus respond to them?

What other works was Jesus doing?

Describing the nature of His works, Acts 10:38 tells us, "*You know of Jesus of Nazareth, how God anointed Him with the Holy Spirit and with power, and how He went about doing good and healing all who were oppressed by the devil, for God was with Him.*" Jesus:

- turned water to wine (John 2:1-11).
- multiplied bread and fish (John 6:1-14).
- caused the blind to see (John 9).
- made a mute man speak (Matthew 9:32-33).
- healed and cleansed leprosy (Matthew 8:1-4).
- healed a paralytic (Mark 2:1-12).
- raised the dead (John 11).
- walked on water (Matthew 14:25-33).
- healed the deaf and those with speech impediments (Mark 7:32-35).
- stilled a great storm (Matthew 8:23-27).
- healed every kind of disease (Matthew 9:35-36).
- cast out demons (Matthew 9:32-33; Mark 1:34).

OBSERVE

If you have the time it's beneficial to look up each of the above passages that reveal the significance of Jesus' works.

No one could do these works but God. These works demonstrate that Jesus came from God and was one with God.

Jesus proved His claim to be the Son of God another way—He lived a sinless life.

Read 1 Peter 1:18-19, 1 Peter 2:22, 2 Corinthians 5:21, and Hebrews 4:15:

- Mark *Christ* and *One* (including pronouns) with a cross. †

1 Peter 1:18-19

18 knowing that you were not redeemed with perishable things like silver or gold from your futile way of life inherited from your forefathers,
19 but with precious blood, as of a lamb unblemished and spotless, *the blood* of Christ.

1 Peter 2:22

22 WHO [CHRIST] COMMITTED NO SIN, NOR WAS ANY DECEIT FOUND IN HIS MOUTH [ISAIAH 53:9];

2 Corinthians 5:21

21 He [God] made Him [Christ] who knew no sin *to be* sin on our behalf, so that we might become the righteousness of God in Him.

Hebrews 4:15

15 For we do not have a high priest [Jesus] who cannot sympathize with our weaknesses, but One who has been tempted in all things as *we are, yet* without sin.

REFLECT

How is Christ described in these passages?

The Heart of The Matter

Let's review what we learned the past two weeks about Jesus of Nazareth, the Messiah (Christ), the Son of God:

- Jesus' genealogy is that of the prophesied Messiah.

- Jesus fulfills all of the other prophecies concerning the Messiah.

- God the Father testified from heaven at Jesus' baptism that He was His beloved Son, in whom He was well-pleased.

- The Holy Spirit testified that Jesus was the Promised One by descending upon Him in the form of a dove at His baptism.

- Jesus' followers identified Him as the Christ, the Son of the Living God.

- Jesus declared Himself to be the Son of God and proved it by doing the works of His Father—preaching, working miracles, signs, and wonders, casting out demons, and forgiving sin.

- Jesus existed from all eternity.

- Jesus lived a sinless life.

What a Messiah! What a Deliverer! What a Savior!

His name is Jesus of Nazareth.

He is the Promised One, the seed of the woman (Genesis 3:15).

He is the Christ, the Son of the living God.

He is Immanuel, God with us!

This week we read that Jesus asked His followers, "Who do you say that I am?" He asks the same question of us today.

Have these truths about Jesus Christ become real to you personally?

How can knowing Jesus bring you peace with God?

Week Seven—*The Opposition, Betrayal, and Arrest of Jesus*

The New Testament contains four eyewitness accounts of Jesus' life. These historical books are called the Gospels: Matthew, Mark, Luke, and John. Each one begins with references to the eagerly anticipated Promised One's coming to earth to fulfill Old Testament prophecies. The Gospels reveal Jesus' relationship to His Father in heaven as that of an obedient Son always seeking to do the will of His Father. The Gospels also give witness to His earthly ministry of teaching, signs, wonders, miracles, and casting out demons. People were astonished by Jesus' profound and powerful life and teaching.

Last week we examined Scriptures that showed that Jesus of Nazareth was the long-awaited Messiah, the Son of God who is one with God. We saw how some Jews responded adversely to Him. This week we will continue to observe how certain individuals and groups of people responded to Jesus.

OBSERVE

Read Mark 3:1-6:

- Mark *Jesus* (including pronouns) with a cross. †

- Underline every reference to ***Pharisees*** (including pronouns).

Mark 3:1-6

1 He [Jesus] entered again into a synagogue; and a man was there whose hand was withered.
2 They [Pharisees] were watching Him *to see* if He would heal him on the Sabbath, so that they might accuse Him.
3 He said to the man with the withered hand, "Get up and come forward!"

4 And He said to them, "Is it lawful to do good or to do harm on the Sabbath, to save a life or to kill?" But they kept silent.

5 After looking around at them with anger, grieved at their hardness of heart, He said to the man, "Stretch out your hand." And he stretched it out, and his hand was restored.

6 The Pharisees went out and immediately *began* conspiring with the Herodians against Him, *as to* how they might destroy Him.

INSIGHT

The Pharisees (a Jewish religious sect) were very zealous in keeping God's commandments. To ensure that they did, they created regulations to carefully define how to keep the Law. For instance, the fourth commandment forbids working on the Sabbath. In defining what it means to work on the Sabbath, the Pharisees developed restrictions such as a limit to walking only a certain distance and to carrying a certain weight. In their slavish obedience to these rules they missed the weightier points of the Law like justice, mercy, and faithfulness (Matthew 23), and they hypocritically laid these "heavy burdens" on everyone else but did not keep them themselves. And as we see in this passage, the Pharisees even considered a physician's healing someone whose life was not in danger to be work, kindling their scorn. But Jesus rejected their hypocrisy.

The Jewish political party called the Herodians (v. 6) defended Roman rule in those days.

REFLECT

What did you learn from marking *Jesus*?

What did you learn from marking *Pharisees*?

OBSERVE

Six days before the Passover Jesus came to the village of Bethany. There a woman named Mary anointed Him. In the next passage compare the response and motivation of some of those who were close to Him.

Read John 12:3-7:

- Mark *Mary* (including pronouns) with an **M**.
- Draw a rectangle around Judas Iscariot (including pronouns).

INSIGHT

At the beginning of Jesus' ministry, He chose twelve disciples who were always with Him, not only learning but also witnessing the miracles and work His Father was doing through Him. Judas Iscariot was among them.

John 12:3-7

3   Mary then took a pound of very costly perfume of pure nard, and anointed the feet of Jesus and wiped His feet with her hair; and the house was filled with the fragrance of the perfume.

4   But Judas Iscariot, one of His disciples, who was intending to betray Him, said,

5   "Why was this perfume not sold for three hundred denarii [300 days' wages], and given to poor *people?*"

6   Now he said this, not because he was concerned about the poor, but because he was a thief, and as he had the money box, he used to pilfer what was put into it.

7   Therefore Jesus said, "Let her alone, so that she may keep it for the day of My burial."

REFLECT

Why did Mary anoint Jesus?

What did you learn about Judas Iscariot?

What was Jesus' response? What did He predict?

OBSERVE

Those who heard Jesus' teaching all faced a choice.

Read John 6:63-64 (Jesus is speaking):

- Mark *Jesus* (including pronouns) with a cross. †

   John 6:63-64

   63 "It is the Spirit who gives life; the flesh profits
      nothing; the words that I have spoken to you are
      spirit and are life.
   64 "But there are some of you who do not believe." For
      Jesus knew from the beginning who they were who
      did not believe, and who it was that would betray
      Him.

REFLECT

What did you learn about Jesus and the people's response to Him?

OBSERVE

Jesus knows the hearts of all men. He knew what was going to happen to Him in the days ahead, and He told His disciples in advance.

Read Matthew 20:17-19:

- Mark *Jesus* and *Son of Man* (including pronouns) with a cross. †

Matthew 20:17-19

17   As Jesus was about to go up to Jerusalem, He took the twelve *disciples* aside by themselves, and on the way He said to them,

18   "Behold, we are going up to Jerusalem; and the Son of Man will be delivered to the chief priests and scribes, and they will condemn Him to death,

19   and will hand Him over to the Gentiles to mock and scourge and crucify *Him,* and on the third day He will be raised up."

REFLECT

What did you learn from marking *Jesus*?

INSIGHT
Five days before the Passover Jesus rode into Jerusalem on a colt, fulfilling the Messianic prophecy of Zechariah 9:9 which was written over 500 years earlier: Rejoice greatly, O daughter of Zion! Shout *in triumph,* O daughter of Jerusalem! Behold, your king is coming to you; He is just and endowed with salvation, Humble, and mounted on a donkey, Even on a colt, the foal of a donkey.

OBSERVE

Read John 12:12-16:

- Mark *Jesus* and *King* (including pronouns) with a cross. †

John 12:12-16

12 On the next day the large crowd who had come to the feast, when they heard that Jesus was coming to Jerusalem,

13 took the branches of the palm trees and went out to meet Him, and *began* to shout, "Hosanna! BLESSED IS HE WHO COMES IN THE NAME OF THE LORD, even the King of Israel" [Psalm 118:26].

14 Jesus, finding a young donkey, sat on it; as it is written,

15 "FEAR NOT, DAUGHTER OF ZION; BEHOLD, YOUR KING IS COMING, SEATED ON A DONKEY'S COLT" [Zechariah 9:9].

16 These things His disciples did not understand at the first; but when Jesus was glorified, then they remembered that these things were written of Him, and that they had done these things to Him.

REFLECT

Describe what happened on this day.

Did the disciples understand what was happening at this time? When did they know?

OBSERVE

Jesus then gave His disciples understanding concerning what was about to take place. He revealed His inner struggle facing the events ahead.

Read the selected verses from John 12 and mark:

- *Jesus* (including titles and pronouns) with a cross. †
- *ruler of this world* with a pitchfork. 𝘺
- *hour* with a clock. ⏰

John 12:23-24, 27-28, 31-33

23 And Jesus answered them, saying, "The hour has come for the Son of Man to be glorified.

24 "Truly, truly, I say to you, unless a grain of wheat falls into the earth and dies, it remains alone; but if it dies, it bears much fruit."

27 "Now My [Jesus'] soul has become troubled; and what shall I say, 'Father, save Me from this hour'? But for this purpose I came to this hour.

28 "Father, glorify Your name." Then a voice came out of heaven: "I have both glorified it, and will glorify it again."

31 "Now judgment is upon this world; now the ruler of this world [Satan] will be cast out.

32 "And I [Jesus], if I am lifted up from the earth, will draw all men to Myself."

33 But He was saying this to indicate the kind of death by which He was to die.

REFLECT

What did you learn by marking the references to *Jesus*?

What did you learn from marking *hour*? What hour was Jesus referring to?

What did you learn from marking *the ruler of this world*?

According to verses 32-33, what kind of death was Jesus indicating that He was about to die? Does this tie back to anything in Genesis 3?

OBSERVE

Let's quickly review what we learned in Week Three.

In the unfolding of His eternal plan, the LORD first promised the Messiah's coming just after man sinned in the garden of Eden (Genesis 3:15).

Read Genesis 3:14-15 and mark:

- *seed* of the woman (including pronouns) with a cross. †
- *serpent* (including pronouns) with a pitchfork. �

Genesis 3:14-15

14 The LORD God said to the serpent,
    "Because you have done this,
       Cursed are you more than all cattle,
       And more than every beast of the field;
       On your belly you will go,
       And dust you will eat
       All the days of your life;
15   And I will put enmity
       Between you and the woman,
       And between your seed and her seed;
       He shall bruise you on the head,
       And you shall bruise him on the heel."

REFLECT

Jesus was coming to the end of His earthly life. What parallels do you see in God's prophecy in Genesis 3:15 and the passages we just read from John 12?

INSIGHT

As Jesus foretold, Roman soldiers nailed his hands and feet to a cross which was then lifted up and put into the ground. As prophesied, crucifixion bruised His heel.

OBSERVE

In this next passage we'll see a conspiracy unfolding, a betrayal planned by one of Jesus' twelve disciples. This betrayal was prophesied in Psalm 41:9: "Even my close friend in whom I trusted, who ate my bread, has lifted up his heel against me."

Read Luke 22:1-8:

- Underline ***chief priests, scribes,*** and ***officers*** (including pronouns).

- Mark ***Judas*** and ***Iscariot*** (including pronouns) with a rectangle. ☐

Luke 22:1-8

1 Now the Feast of Unleavened Bread, which is called the Passover, was approaching.

2 The chief priests and the scribes were seeking how they might put Him [Jesus] to death; for they were afraid of the people.

3 And Satan entered into Judas who was called Iscariot, belonging to the number of the twelve.

4 And he went away and discussed with the chief priests and officers how he might betray Him to them.

5 They were glad and agreed to give him money.

6 So he consented, and *began* seeking a good opportunity to betray Him to them apart from the crowd.

7 Then came the *first* day of Unleavened Bread on which the Passover *lamb* had to be sacrificed.

8 And Jesus sent Peter and John, saying, "Go and prepare the Passover for us, so that we may eat it."

REFLECT

What did you learn from marking *chief priests, scribes,* and *officers*?

What did you learn from marking *Judas*?

According to verses 1 and 7, when did the events described take place?

OBSERVE

During the last supper Jesus washed His disciples' feet and told them that one of them will betray Him.

Read John 13:21, 25-27:

- Draw a rectangle around *Judas* and *one* (including pronouns and synonyms). ☐
- Mark *Satan* with a pitchfork. Ψ

John 13:21, 25-27

21 When Jesus had said this, He became troubled in spirit, and testified and said, "Truly, truly, I say to you, that one of you will betray Me."

25 He [John], leaning back thus on Jesus' bosom, said to Him, "Lord, who is it?"

26 Jesus then answered, "That is the one for whom I shall dip the morsel and give it to him." So when He had dipped the morsel, He took and gave it to Judas, *the son* of Simon Iscariot.

27 After the morsel, Satan then entered into him [Judas]. Therefore Jesus said to him, "What you do, do quickly."

REFLECT

What did you learn from marking *Judas*?

OBSERVE

Immediately after this Passover meal, knowing His time was short and that the Scriptures concerning His death were about to be fulfilled, Jesus went with His disciples to the garden of Gethsemane to pray.

Read the selected verses from Matthew 26:

- Mark *Jesus* (including all titles and pronouns) with a cross. ✝

- Draw a rectangle around Judas (including all synonyms and pronouns).

Matthew 26:36-39, 42, 44-50

36 Then Jesus came with them to a place called Gethsemane, and said to His disciples, "Sit here while I go over there and pray."

37 And He took with Him Peter and the two sons of Zebedee, and began to be grieved and distressed.

38 Then He said to them, "My soul is deeply grieved, to the point of death; remain here and keep watch with Me."

39 And He went a little beyond *them,* and fell on His face and prayed, saying, "My Father, if it is possible, let this cup [cup of God's wrath against sin] pass from Me; yet not as I will, but as You will."

42 He went away again a second time and prayed, saying, "My Father, if this cannot pass away unless I drink it, Your will be done."

44 And He left them again, and went away and prayed a third time, saying the same thing once more.

45 Then He came to the disciples and said to them, "Are you still sleeping and resting? Behold, the hour is at hand and the Son of Man is being betrayed into the hands of sinners.

46 "Get up, let us be going; behold, the one who betrays Me is at hand!"

47 While He was still speaking, behold, Judas, one of the twelve, came up accompanied by a large crowd with swords and clubs, *who came* from the chief priests and elders of the people.

48 Now he who was betraying Him gave them a sign, saying, "Whomever I kiss, He is the one; seize Him."

49 Immediately Judas went to Jesus and said, "Hail, Rabbi!" and kissed Him.

50 And Jesus said to him, "Friend, *do* what you have come for." Then they came and laid hands on Jesus and seized Him.

REFLECT

What did you learn from marking *Judas*?

What did you learn from marking *Jesus*? How did He respond to Judas' betrayal?

The Heart of The Matter

Not everyone believed Jesus and the promises of God. This week we observed the events that led to Jesus' betrayal during the last week of His life on earth. In this lesson we learned:

- The Pharisees planned to kill Jesus.

- Mary anointed Jesus for burial.

- Jesus foretold His betrayal, death, and resurrection to His disciples.

- Jesus fulfilled Zechariah's prophecy of the Messiah riding into Jerusalem on a colt.

- The hour had come for Jesus to be crucified.

- Judas Iscariot betrayed Jesus.

- Jesus did not want to face suffering, death, and separation from His Father, but He submitted to His Father's will.

After living a perfect, sinless life on earth, Jesus made the ultimate sacrifice—willingly laying down His life to pay in full the penalty for our sins, making it possible for sinners to be brought into a right relationship with God.

This is God's way, the *only* way to have peace with Him.

Have you considered what Jesus faced to make it possible for you to have peace with God?

Week Eight—*The Trials and Crucifixion of Jesus*

In Week Seven we observed Scriptures concerning the conspiracy to betray Jesus. After Judas's betrayal, Jesus was subjected to a number of trials. The Jews tried Him three times. The first trial was before Annas, the former high priest, the second before the presiding high priest Caiaphas and the Sanhedrin (the Jewish rulers), and the third before the Sanhedrin which passed a death sentence on Him. Enraged they spat in His face, beat Him with their fists, and slapped Him (Matthew 26:67). Since the Sanhedrin did not have the authority to put anyone to death, Jesus' opponents had to accuse him of a crime worthy of death before Roman governors.

Jesus also faced three Roman trials: before Pontius Pilate (the Roman Governor of Judea), before Herod Antipas (the Roman puppet ruler of Galilee), and then, again, before Pilate. Despite his wife's warning and knowing that Jesus was innocent, Pilate sentenced Jesus to death by crucifixion.

While in Roman hands Jesus was scourged, had a crown of thorns embedded in His head, was mocked, spat upon, beaten, and crucified between two criminals.

With this overview in mind, this week we will observe two of His trials and examine His death and its implications.

OBSERVE

Let's begin with the second Jewish trial.

Read Mark 14:55-64:

- Mark *Jesus* (including all titles and pronouns) with a cross. †

Mark 14:55-64

55 Now the chief priests and the whole Council [Sanhedrin] kept trying to obtain testimony against Jesus to put Him to death, and they were not finding any.

56 For many were giving false testimony against Him, but their testimony was not consistent.

57 Some stood up and *began* to give false testimony against Him, saying,

58 "We heard Him say, 'I will destroy this temple made with hands, and in three days I will build another made without hands.'"

59 Not even in this respect was their testimony consistent.

60 The high priest [Caiaphas] stood up *and came* forward and questioned Jesus, saying, "Do You not answer? What is it that these men are testifying against You?"

61 But He kept silent and did not answer. Again the high priest was questioning Him, and saying to Him, "Are You the Christ, the Son of the Blessed *One?*"

62 And Jesus said, "I am; and you shall see THE SON OF MAN SITTING AT THE RIGHT HAND OF POWER, and COMING WITH THE CLOUDS OF HEAVEN" [Psalm 110:1; Daniel 7:13].

63 Tearing his clothes, the high priest said, "What further need do we have of witnesses?

64 "You have heard the blasphemy; how does it seem to you?" And they all condemned Him to be deserving of death.

REFLECT

From marking *Jesus*, what did you learn about the charges against Him and His response?

INSIGHT

The testimony against Jesus regarding the temple (v. 58) was a misunderstanding of what He said at the beginning of His ministry. When Jesus cleansed the temple of the moneychangers, they asked Him for a sign to prove His authority to do so. Jesus replied, "'Destroy this temple, and in three days I will raise it up.' The Jews then said, 'It took forty-six years to build this temple, and will You raise it up in three days?' But He was speaking of the temple of His body" (John 2:19-21). Jesus was not referring to the temple in Jerusalem, but He was prophesying to them that He would be bodily resurrected in three days.

To understand the significance of Jesus' answer in verse 62, Old Testament background is necessary. In Exodus 3:1-15, the LORD God appeared to Moses at the burning bush and told him to go back to Egypt to deliver His people. Moses asked the LORD whom should he say sent him. The LORD responded, "I AM WHO I AM." He was to say, "'I AM has sent me to you.'" By Jesus' responding "I am," He was undeniably claiming to be the true God.

What is Jesus declaring in verse 62 when He answers the question, "Are you the Christ [Messiah], the Son of the Blessed One?"

According to verses 63-64, how did the high priest, knowing the significance of "I AM," respond to Jesus' claim?

OBSERVE

Now let's look at Jesus' last Roman trial before Pilate.

Read John 19:1-14 and mark:

- *Jesus* (including all titles and pronouns) with a cross. †

- *Pilate* (including pronouns) with a **P**.

John 19:1-14

1 Pilate then took Jesus and scourged Him.

2 And the soldiers twisted together a crown of thorns and put it on His head, and put a purple robe on Him;

3 and they *began* to come up to Him and say, "Hail, King of the Jews!" and to give Him slaps *in the face.*

4 Pilate came out again and said to them, "Behold, I am bringing Him out to you so that you may know that I find no guilt in Him."

5 Jesus then came out, wearing the crown of thorns and the purple robe. *Pilate* said to them, "Behold, the Man!"

6 So when the chief priests and the officers saw Him, they cried out saying, "Crucify, crucify!" Pilate said to them, "Take Him yourselves and crucify Him, for I find no guilt in Him."

7 The Jews answered him, "We have a law, and by that law He ought to die because He made Himself out *to be* the Son of God."

8 Therefore when Pilate heard this statement, he was *even* more afraid;

9 and he entered into the Praetorium again and said to Jesus, "Where are You from?" But Jesus gave him no answer.

10 So Pilate said to Him, "You do not speak to me? Do You not know that I have authority to release You, and I have authority to crucify You?"

11 Jesus answered, "You would have no authority over Me, unless it had been given you from above; for this reason he who delivered Me to you has *the* greater sin."

12 As a result of this Pilate made efforts to release Him, but the Jews cried out saying, "If you release this Man, you are no friend of Caesar; everyone who makes himself out *to be* a king opposes Caesar."

13 Therefore when Pilate heard these words, he brought Jesus out, and sat down on the judgment seat at a place called The Pavement, but in Hebrew, Gabbatha.

14 Now it was the day of preparation for the Passover; it was about the sixth hour. And he said to the Jews, "Behold, your King!"

INSIGHT

The tool used for scourging (John 19:1) was a short whip with braided leather thongs of different lengths, each having small iron or lead balls, rocks, or sharp bone fragments attached. Pain and blood loss from scourging were severe.

REFLECT

Review the events that took place in John 19:1-14.

According to verses 4 and 6, what was Pilate's verdict?

What law were the Jews accusing Jesus of breaking that was worthy of death?

Describe Jesus' appearance in verse 5.

According to verse 6, how did the chief priests and officers respond?

According to verse 11, what did Jesus say with regard to Pilate's authority?

From what you saw in verses 12 and 13, why did Pilate finally deliver Jesus to death?

The Jews rejected Jesus as their Messiah. In what ways do people still reject Him today?

INSIGHT

Jesus was clear in His claim to be the Christ, the Son of God. Why were the Jews, who had been looking for their promised Messiah for 4,000 years, so adamant in rejecting Him?

To understand the answer to this question, we need to think back over all the Messianic prophecies we observed in Week Four. These prophecies fall into two main categories: the Suffering Servant/Lamb of God (Isaiah 53) and the Reigning King (Isaiah 9:6-7, Daniel 7:13-14, Jeremiah 23:5).

Jesus lived in Israel when His people were suffering under heavy Roman domination. The Jews were looking for their prophesied Messiah to come as King to overthrow the Romans and set up His kingdom. At one point after Jesus fed the 5,000, some Jews tried to take Him by force to make Him their king; but Jesus knew the time was not right, so He withdrew to a mountain to be alone (John 6:15). Looking for the King, they did not recognize the Suffering Servant, the Lamb of God who had to come first to take away the sins of the world.

Jesus, the King of kings and Lord of lords, *is* coming again. When He does, Jews will look on Him whom they pierced (Zechariah 12:10) and mourn for Him.

OBSERVE

Despite protests from the chief priests, on the cross above His head, Pilate wrote the charge against Him, "THIS IS JESUS THE KING OF THE JEWS" (Matthew 27:37). It was written in three languages (Hebrew, Greek, and Latin) so most people could read it.

Read John 19:17-19, 23-24:

- Mark *Jesus* (including all titles and pronouns) with a cross. †

John 19:17-19, 23-24

17 They took Jesus, therefore, and He went out, bearing His own cross, to the place called the Place of a Skull, which is called in Hebrew, Golgotha.

18 There they crucified Him, and with Him two other men, one on either side, and Jesus in between.

19 Pilate also wrote an inscription and put it on the cross. It was written, "JESUS THE NAZARENE, THE KING OF THE JEWS."

23 Then the soldiers, when they had crucified Jesus, took His outer garments and made four parts, a part to every soldier and *also* the tunic; now the tunic was seamless, woven in one piece.

24 So they said to one another, "Let us not tear it, but cast lots for it, *to decide* whose it shall be"; *this was* to fulfill the Scripture: "THEY DIVIDED MY OUTER GARMENTS AMONG THEM, AND FOR MY CLOTHING THEY CAST LOTS" [Psalm 22:18].

REFLECT

What did you learn from marking *Jesus*?

OBSERVE

Psalm 22 is a prophetic Psalm about the Promised One, the Messiah. It gives over a dozen prophetic details of the crucifixion including Christ's crying out, "My God, my God, why have You forsaken me?" It also speaks of:

- His being reproached and despised by men.
- His being mocked and scorned.
- His bones being out of joint.
- His tongue cleaving to His jaw.
- His hands and feet being pierced.

INSIGHT

Before crucifixion, a criminal was nailed through his wrists to a horizontal crossbar. His feet were then nailed to a vertical shaft with his knees bent, enabling him to push up with his legs in order to breathe (bruising his heel: Genesis 3:15). This produced excruciating pain. Falling back down scraped his raw back each time. If Roman executors wanted to speed up death, they could break a criminal's legs so he would quickly suffocate.

Jesus the Lamb of God died at the same time the Passover lambs were being sacrificed in the temple. He died as THE Passover Lamb as 1 Corinthians 5:7b tells us—"...Christ our Passover also has been sacrificed."

On the day Jesus was crucified darkness fell upon all the land from the sixth to the ninth hour. About the ninth hour, while suffering the agonies of the crucifixion, Jesus spoke seven times (Matthew 27:45-46):

- to His Father for those who crucified Him: "Father, forgive them; for they do not know what they are doing" (Luke 23:33-34).

- to the believing thief hanging on a cross next to Him: "Truly I say to you, today you shall be with Me in Paradise" (Luke 23:43).

- to His mother and to John, His disciple: "Woman, behold, your son!" and "Behold, your mother!" (John 19:26-27).

- to His Father: "MY GOD, MY GOD, WHY HAVE YOU FORSAKEN ME?" (Matthew 27:46; Psalm 22:1).

- to those near the cross: "I am thirsty" (John 19:28).

- to His Father and to the world, a declaration of triumph: "It is finished!" (John 19:30).

- to His Father: "'Father, INTO YOUR HANDS I COMMIT MY SPIRIT.' Having said this, He breathed His last" (Luke 23:46; Psalm 31:5).

REFLECT

Facing imminent death on the cross, what do you think was on Jesus' heart based on what He said?

What additional insights did you glean about Jesus and His love from His last sayings? What words impacted you most? Why?

> ### INSIGHT
>
> With His own blood Jesus paid in full the ultimate price for our redemption. He laid down His life willingly as full payment for the sins of the world.
>
> On the cross He became our substitute, dying in our place to save us from our sins. He credited our death to His account and His righteousness to ours, justifying and reconciling us (bringing us back into right relationship) to God.

OBSERVE

What events followed after Jesus gave up His spirit (life)?

Read Matthew 27:50-51:

- Mark *Jesus* (including pronouns) with a cross. †

Matthew 27:50-51

50 And Jesus cried out again with a loud voice, and yielded up His spirit.
51 And behold, the veil of the temple was torn in two from top to bottom; and the earth shook and the rocks were split.

> ### INSIGHT
>
> The temple veil was an extremely thick, finely embroidered, woven material that separated the Holy Place from the Holy of Holies. It was here where God had chosen to dwell with man. Even the priests did not have free access to the presence of God; only the high priest, with sacrificial blood, could enter this inner chamber once a year.
>
> *(continued on next page)*

INSIGHT (continued)
At the moment of Jesus' death, the veil in the temple was torn "from top to bottom." This was to signify that there was no longer a separation between God and man. The shed blood of Jesus Christ had now opened the way into a new and living relationship with God (see Hebrews 10:19-20). Now, whoever chose to come to God by way of the shed blood of the Cross would have access into the very Holy of Holies (God's presence) to fellowship with Him.

Read John 19:31-37:

- Mark *Jesus* (including pronouns) with a cross. †

John 19:31-37

31 Then the Jews, because it was the day of preparation, so that the bodies would not remain on the cross on the Sabbath (for that Sabbath was a high day), asked Pilate that their legs might be broken, and *that* they might be taken away.

32 So the soldiers came, and broke the legs of the first man and of the other who was crucified with Him;

33 but coming to Jesus, when they saw that He was already dead, they did not break His legs.

34 But one of the soldiers pierced His side with a spear, and immediately blood and water came out.

35 And he who has seen has testified, and his testimony is true; and he knows that he is telling the truth, so that you also may believe.

36 For these things came to pass to fulfill the Scripture, "NOT A BONE OF HIM SHALL BE BROKEN" [Psalm 34:20].

37 And again another Scripture says, "THEY SHALL LOOK ON HIM WHOM THEY PIERCED" [Zechariah 12:10].

REFLECT

What did you learn from marking *Jesus*?

From Matthew's account, what happened the moment Jesus died?

Why didn't the soldiers break Jesus' legs? What promise did this fulfill? Where is it found?

INSIGHT
When Jesus was crucified He shed His blood. This is very significant because Leviticus 17:11a states, "For the life of the flesh is in the blood, and I have given it to you on the altar to make atonement for your souls;"

INSIGHT
Sin is a serious offense against God that alienates and separates man from Him. Sin's gravity is seen in the fact that its penalty is death (wages, Romans 6:23). The penalty must be paid to bring man back into right relationship (peace) with God. Old Testament sacrifices pointed to Christ and provided a temporary covering for sin, delaying the penalty, but the ultimate debt still needed to be paid. Christ's death paid the final penalty for sin and satisfied God's justice. Without Jesus' substitutionary death, His shedding of blood, there could be no forgiveness for man's sins and no peace with God.

OBSERVE

Read Hebrews 9:22:

Hebrews 9:22

22 And according to the Law, *one may* almost *say*, all things are cleansed with blood, and without shedding of blood there is no forgiveness.

REFLECT

What did you learn about being cleansed from sin and forgiven?

OBSERVE

Though we are unworthy sinners, God demonstrated His love for us by sending Christ to satisfy His justice.

INSIGHT
In Hebrews 2:17 (see the passage below), the Greek word for **propitiation** means *to satisfy* or *appease*. What is satisfied? God's holiness. What is appeased? God's righteous wrath against sin.

Read 2 Corinthians 5:21 and Hebrews 2:9-10, 14-18 and mark:

- *Jesus* and *author* (including pronouns) with a cross. †
- the *devil* (including pronouns) with a pitchfork. ⩚
- *death* with a tombstone. ⬀

2 Corinthians 5:21

21 He [God the Father] made Him [Jesus] who knew no sin *to be* sin on our behalf, so that we might become the righteousness of God in Him.

Hebrews 2:9-10, 14-18

9 But we do see Him who was made for a little while lower than the angels, *namely,* Jesus, because of the suffering of death crowned with glory and honor, so that by the grace of God He might taste death for everyone.

10 For it was fitting for Him [God], for whom are all things, and through whom are all things, in bringing many sons to glory, to perfect the author of their salvation through sufferings.

14 Therefore, since the children share in flesh and blood, He [Jesus] Himself likewise also partook of the same, that through death He might render powerless him who had the power of death, that is, the devil,

15 and might free those who through fear of death were subject to slavery all their lives.

16 For assuredly He does not give help to angels, but He gives help to the descendant of Abraham.

17 Therefore, He had to be made like His brethren in all things, so that He might become a merciful and faithful high priest in things pertaining to God, to make propitiation for the sins of the people.

18 For since He Himself was tempted in that which He has suffered, He is able to come to the aid of those who are tempted.

REFLECT

What did you learn about Jesus?

According to Hebrews 2:14-15, why did Jesus become flesh and blood?

Why was Jesus made like His brethren in all things (Hebrews 2:17)?

How does 2 Corinthians 5:21 relate to this?

Was Jesus made sin for you? Why?

INSIGHT
From these passages we learn that Jesus laid aside His glory, became a man, lived a sinless life, took our sins upon Him, and died as our propitiation (satisfying God's holiness), taking upon Himself and enduring the holy wrath sin demands. He paid the full penalty of our sin, "the wages of sin" we owed. He totally defeated Satan and took away his power over us (1 John 3:8). In His great sacrifice, He crushed the serpent's head even as His own heel was bruised (Genesis 3:15).

After reading through this week's study, what stood out or was personally meaningful for you?

The Heart of The Matter

Have you considered how the events surrounding Jesus' death changed history?

From the hastily called trials to the crucifixion of Jesus Christ, we have learned that:

- Jesus faced three Jewish and three Roman trials.

- Pontius Pilate sentenced Jesus to scourging and death by crucifixion, despite knowing Jesus was innocent.

- Every detail of Jesus' crucifixion fulfilled prophecy.

- Jesus died as the Lamb of God at the same time that the high priest's Passover lamb was being sacrificed.

- Sinners were offered mercy they did not deserve, and God's justice was satisfied.

- Jesus' death made propitiation for the sins of the world (1 John 2:2), and opened the way for man to have peace with God.

*Greater love has no one than this, that one lay down
his life for his friends.*
JOHN 15:13

*I [Jesus] am the good shepherd; the good shepherd lays down
His life for the sheep.*
JOHN 10:11

*For this reason the Father loves Me, because I lay down My life
so that I may take it again. No one has taken it away from Me, but I lay
it down on My own initiative. I have authority to lay it down, and I have
authority to take it up again...*
JOHN 10:17-18a

We know love by this, that He laid down His life for us....
1 JOHN 3:16a

By this the love of God was manifested in us, that God has sent His only begotten Son into the world so that we might live through Him. In this is love, not that we loved God, but that He loved us and sent His Son to be *the propitiation for our sins.*
1 JOHN 4:9-10

How have these truths changed your life?

What is the most significant insight you have learned from this week's study?

Week Nine—*Jesus Christ's Burial and Resurrection*

Man unjustly crucified Jesus Christ, but it was God's predetermined plan that Jesus would lay down His life voluntarily, shedding His blood for the propitiation and forgiveness of our sins. In love, God sent His Son to pay the penalty we could not pay, satisfying His holiness and justice. Resolved to do God's will, Jesus went willingly to the cross as He said: "No one has taken it [My life] away from Me, but I lay it down on My own initiative. I have authority to lay it down, and I have authority to take it up again. This commandment I received from My Father" (John 10:18).

This week we will see how Jesus fulfilled God's eternal plan: dying on the cross, being buried, rising from the dead, and ascending to His Father.

Let's look at Jesus' burial.

OBSERVE

What happened after the crucifixion?

Read John 19:38-42:

- Mark ***Jesus*** (including pronouns) with a cross. †

   John 19:38-42

   38 After these things [the crucifixion] Joseph of Arimathea, being a disciple of Jesus, but a secret *one* for fear of the Jews, asked Pilate that he might take away the body of Jesus; and Pilate granted permission. So he came and took away His body.

   39 Nicodemus, who had first come to Him by night [John 3:1-21], also came, bringing a mixture of myrrh and aloes, about a hundred pounds *weight*.

40 So they took the body of Jesus and bound it in linen wrappings with the spices, as is the burial custom of the Jews.

41 Now in the place where He was crucified there was a garden, and in the garden a new tomb in which no one had yet been laid.

42 Therefore because of the Jewish day of preparation, since the tomb was nearby, they laid Jesus there.

REFLECT

What did you learn about Jesus and His burial?

OBSERVE

After the chief priests and Pharisees saw Jesus crucified, they were still concerned. Let's see why.

Read Matthew 27:62-66:

- Underline ***chief priests*** and the ***Pharisees*** (including pronouns).

- Mark ***Pilate*** and ***Sir*** with a **P**.

- Mark ***Jesus*** (including ***He, I, Him*** and synonyms) with a cross. †

Matthew 27:62-66

62 Now on the next day, the day after the preparation, the chief priests and the Pharisees gathered together with Pilate,

63 and said, "Sir, we remember that when He [Jesus] was still alive that deceiver said, 'After three days I *am* to rise again.'

64 "Therefore, give orders for the grave to be made secure until the third day, otherwise His disciples may come and steal Him away and say to the people, 'He has risen from the dead,' and the last deception will be worse than the first."

65 Pilate said to them, "You have a guard; go, make it *as* secure as you know how."

66 And they went and made the grave secure, and along with the guard they set a seal on the stone [which blocked the entrance to the tomb].

REFLECT

Why did the chief priests and Pharisees go to Pilate?

How did Pilate respond to the chief priests' and Pharisees' request?

INSIGHT

This Roman guard was probably a division of sixteen men who rotated every six hours in groups of four. The four were called a *quaternion*. This rotation guaranteed that the four on duty would be alert and ready for anything. The twelve other men stationed nearby would be preparing for their shift by sleeping or eating. Sleeping on guard duty was punishable by death, not only for the sleeping guard but also for those on duty with him.

To seal a tomb as Pilate directed, it is believed that a cord or piece of rawhide was drawn across the stone and attached on both sides with clay or wax, which was impressed with the seal of Rome. The penalty for unauthorized breaking of this seal was death.

In all these attempts to prevent Christ's prophesied resurrection, the enemies of Jesus Christ unknowingly provided corroborative evidence for it.

INSIGHT

The death and resurrection of Jesus Christ were not just historical events; they were also central to God's eternal plan and the fulfillment of numerous Old Testament prophecies. We saw in Matthew 20:17-19 (Week 7) that Jesus prophesied His condemnation, mocking, scourging, crucifixion, and resurrection on the third day.

OBSERVE

Now let's look at Matthew's account of the resurrection.

Read Matthew 28:1-15 and mark:

- *Jesus* (including pronouns) with a cross. †

- the **women** (including names and pronouns) with a circle.

- **guard, guards,** and **soldiers** (including pronouns) with a **G.**

Matthew 28:1-15

1 Now after the Sabbath, as it began to dawn toward the first *day* of the week, Mary Magdalene and the other Mary came to look at the grave.

2 And behold, a severe earthquake had occurred, for an angel of the Lord descended from heaven and came and rolled away the stone and sat upon it.

3 And his appearance was like lightning, and his clothing as white as snow.

4 The guards shook for fear of him and became like dead men.

5 The angel said to the women, "Do not be afraid; for I know that you are looking for Jesus who has been crucified.

6 "He is not here, for He has risen, just as He said. Come, see the place where He was lying.

7 "Go quickly and tell His disciples that He has risen from the dead; and behold, He is going ahead of you into Galilee, there you will see Him; behold, I have told you."

8 And they left the tomb quickly with fear and great joy and ran to report it to His disciples.

9 And behold, Jesus met them and greeted them. And they came up and took hold of His feet and worshiped Him.

10 Then Jesus said to them, "Do not be afraid; go and take word to My brethren to leave for Galilee, and there they will see Me."

11 Now while they were on their way, some of the guard came into the city and reported to the chief priests all that had happened.

12 And when they had assembled with the elders and consulted together, they gave a large sum of money to the soldiers,

13 and said, "You are to say, 'His disciples came by night and stole Him away while we were asleep.'

14 "And if this should come to the governor's ears, we will win him over and keep you out of trouble."

15 And they took the money and did as they had been instructed; and this story was widely spread among the Jews, *and is* to this day.

REFLECT

What did you learn from marking the *women*? What did the angel say to them? How did they respond to the angel and to Jesus?

What did you learn from marking *Jesus*?

What did you learn from marking *guard*?

Why was sharing the good news of Jesus' resurrection so important?

INSIGHT

The Roman government could easily have put all claims of the resurrection to rest by producing Jesus' body, but they didn't because they were unable to find it. They never did, and never could, because Christ had risen from the dead!

The case for the physical resurrection of Jesus Christ is strong and convincing. Over the years some unbelieving intellectuals set out to disprove the resurrection. Instead, they concluded not only that Christ rose from the dead but also that He was Lord and Savior.

OBSERVE

The Gospels all record Jesus' appearing to the women, to His disciples, and to many after His resurrection. In Luke 24:13-35 Jesus appeared to two of His disciples discouraged by His crucifixion. He lovingly rebuked them. The next passage tells us what He said.

Read Luke 24:25-27:

- Mark *Christ* (including pronouns) with a cross. †

Luke 24:25-27

25 And He [Jesus Christ] said to them, "O foolish men and slow of heart to believe in all that the prophets have spoken!

26 "Was it not necessary for the Christ to suffer these things and to enter into His glory?"

27 Then beginning with Moses and with all the prophets, He explained to them the things concerning Himself in all the Scriptures.

REFLECT

What did you learn from marking *Christ*?

What is the value of studying the Scriptures that point to Christ as we have been doing?

OBSERVE

This next passage gives the last words of the risen Christ before He ascended to heaven.

Read Acts 1:1-11:

- Mark *Jesus* and *Lord* (including pronouns) with a cross. †

Acts 1:1-11

1 The first account I [Luke] composed, Theophilus, about all that Jesus began to do and teach,

2 until the day when He was taken up *to heaven,* after He had by the Holy Spirit given orders to the apostles whom He had chosen.

3 To these He also presented Himself alive after His suffering, by many convincing proofs, appearing to them over *a period of* forty days and speaking of the things concerning the kingdom of God.

4 Gathering them together, He commanded them not to leave Jerusalem, but to wait for what the Father had promised, "Which," *He said,* "you heard of from Me;

5 for John baptized with water, but you will be baptized with the Holy Spirit not many days from now."

6 So when they had come together, they were asking Him, saying, "Lord, is it at this time You are restoring the kingdom to Israel?"

7 He said to them, "It is not for you to know times or epochs which the Father has fixed by His own authority;

8 but you will receive power when the Holy Spirit has come upon you; and you shall be My witnesses both in Jerusalem, and in all Judea and Samaria, and even to the remotest part of the earth."

9 And after He had said these things, He was lifted up while they were looking on, and a cloud received Him out of their sight.

10 And as they were gazing intently into the sky while He was going, behold, two men in white clothing stood beside them.

11 They also said, "Men of Galilee, why do you stand looking into the sky? This Jesus, who has been taken up from you into heaven, will come in just the same way as you have watched Him go into heaven."

REFLECT

What did you learn from marking *Jesus*?

How did Jesus equip and enable His disciples to be His witnesses?

INSIGHT

Luke 24:45-49, a cross-reference to Acts 1:8, says, "Then He [Jesus] opened their [the disciples'] minds to understand the Scriptures, and He said to them, 'Thus it is written, that the Christ would suffer and rise again from the dead the third day, and that repentance for forgiveness of sins would be proclaimed in His name to all the nations, beginning from Jerusalem. You are witnesses of these things. And behold, I am sending forth the promise of My Father upon you; but you are to stay in the city [Jerusalem] until you are clothed with power from on high.'"

Just as Jesus walked on earth in the power of the Holy Spirit, His disciples were called to be His witnesses and to live their lives dependent upon and empowered by His Spirit. We will study the Holy Spirit in more detail in the weeks ahead.

The Heart of The Matter

What appeared to be the darkest, irreversible event in human history, the crucifixion of the sinless Lamb of God, was actually God's way to bring us back to Himself.

This week we saw that:

- Jesus was anointed and buried in a rich man's tomb (Matthew 27:57-60).

- Jesus rose from the dead and appeared to many.

- The chief priests and guards conspired to cover up the resurrection of Jesus.

- After appearing to over 500 brethren (1 Corinthians 15:6) over a period of forty days, Jesus ascended to heaven, promising the gift of His Spirit to enable believers to live out and proclaim God's truth.

Jesus' death, burial, and resurrection prove that He was the long-awaited Messiah, the Christ, the Son of God.

His death verifies His humanity. His victory over death authenticates eternal life. His resurrection proves He is God and that God accepted His payment for sin on our behalf.

Some religions and people claim that Jesus was *just* a good teacher and a prophet. From all that you have learned, what do you believe?

Week Ten—*What is the Gospel?*

For the past nine weeks we have been gaining a greater understanding of how man can have peace with God. God's plan to accomplish this is called the Gospel.

What is the Gospel? The Greek word for **gospel** means *good news.* To understand this good news, we first had to establish the bad news that man rebelled and sinned against his Creator. The instant Adam disobeyed God he died spiritually. Physical death was set into motion; it was just a matter of time. Most significantly, man came under God's judgment for sin. Eternal death, separation from God forever, awaited him. Sin brought rebelliousness, selfishness, meaninglessness, hopelessness, and loneliness into man's existence. Choosing to come out from under God's authority and to live independently, man was alienated from God, becoming an enemy of God, totally incapable of redeeming himself.

From the very beginning, we saw that the LORD God foreknew man's rebellious heart; but in His love and mercy, He promised fallen man a Messiah, a Deliverer, a Savior from the seed of the woman. From before creation, He planned to save man from his sin and its penalty, eternal death. For approximately 4,000 years the LORD sought man, speaking through the Hebrew prophets, repeating and amplifying many, many times over this promise of the Messiah. With each Messianic promise, the LORD God showed man another aspect of who this Messiah would be, where He would come from, what He would do, how He would suffer, how He would save men from their sin, and how He would one day rule over them as their eternal King.

We also learned that the Promised One fulfilled every prophecy in the Bible concerning Himself and His first coming. He was Jesus of Nazareth, the Lamb of God, the Son of Man, the Son of God, and Immanuel—God with us. His sacrificial death was not an accident but the essential part (pivotal event) of God's eternal plan. Despite man's unworthiness, Jesus came to earth "...to seek and to save that which was lost" (Luke 19:10b), to die for the sin of all men, and to rise again from the dead.

This week we will examine the primary passages concerning the Gospel, the good news about Jesus Christ. How should we respond to this Gospel?

OBSERVE

Let's look at one of the clearest definitions of the Gospel in the Scriptures given by the Apostle Paul who wrote the majority of the letters in the New Testament.

Read 1 Corinthians 15:1-8:

- Circle *gospel* and *word* (including pronouns).
- Mark *Christ* (including pronouns) with a cross. †
- Underline the phrase ***according to the Scriptures***.

1 Corinthians 15:1-8

1 Now I [Paul] make known to you, brethren, the gospel which I preached to you, which also you received, in which also you stand,

2 by which also you are saved, if you hold fast the word which I preached to you, unless you believed in vain.

3 For I delivered to you as of first importance what I also received, that ①Christ died for our sins according to the Scriptures,

4 and that He was buried, and that He was raised on the third day according to the Scriptures,

5 and that He appeared to Cephas, then to the twelve.

6 After that He appeared to more than five hundred brethren at one time, most of whom remain until now, but some have fallen asleep;

7 then He appeared to James, then to all the apostles;

8 and last of all, as to one untimely born, He appeared to me also.

REFLECT

What did you learn from marking *gospel*?

What did you learn from marking *Christ*?

What are the main points of the Gospel? Number them in the text. Number one (①) is done for you.

How do verses 5-8 validate the resurrection of Jesus Christ?

The phrase *according to the Scriptures* tells us that Jesus Christ fulfilled prophecy. These prophecies were recorded in the Old Testament over thousands of years.

OBSERVE

Let's look at another passage of Scripture to learn more about the Gospel.

Read Romans 1:1-4, 15-16:

- Mark ***Christ*** and ***Son*** (including pronouns and titles) with a cross. †
- Circle ***gospel*** (including pronouns).

Romans 1:1-4, 15-16

1 Paul, a bond-servant of Christ Jesus, called *as* an apostle, set apart for the gospel of God,

2 which He promised beforehand through His prophets in the holy Scriptures,

3 concerning His Son, who was born of a descendant of David according to the flesh,

4 who was declared the Son of God with power by the resurrection from the dead, according to the Spirit of holiness, Jesus Christ our Lord,

15 So, for my part, I am eager to preach the gospel to you also who are in Rome.
16 For I am not ashamed of the gospel, for it is the power of God for salvation to everyone who believes, to the Jew first and also to the Greek.

REFLECT

What did you learn from marking *Christ*?

What did you learn from marking *gospel*?

What does the Gospel bring to everyone who believes?

OBSERVE

Recall that in Genesis 12 (Week 3) God promised Abraham that in him all nations of the earth would be blessed. The Gospel was not just for the Jews; Gentiles also could find salvation through faith in the death and resurrection of Jesus.

In this next passage Peter preached the Gospel to the first Gentile to believe in Jesus, Cornelius, a Roman centurion (a military officer commanding 100 soldiers).

Read Acts 10:36-43:

- Mark *Jesus* (including all titles and pronouns) with a cross. †
- Put a cloud around *peace.*
- Underline *believes*.

Acts 10:36-43

36 "The word which He [God] sent to the sons of Israel, preaching peace through Jesus Christ (He is Lord of all)—

37 you yourselves know the thing which took place throughout all Judea, starting from Galilee, after the baptism which John proclaimed.

38 "*You know of* Jesus of Nazareth, how God anointed Him with the Holy Spirit and with power, and *how* He went about doing good and healing all who were oppressed by the devil, for God was with Him.

39 "We are witnesses of all the things He did both in the land of the Jews and in Jerusalem. They also put Him to death by hanging Him on a cross.

40 "God raised Him up on the third day and granted that He become visible,

41 not to all the people, but to witnesses who were chosen beforehand by God, *that is,* to us who ate and drank with Him after He arose from the dead.

42 "And He ordered us to preach to the people, and solemnly to testify that this is the One who has been appointed by God as Judge of the living and the dead.

43 "Of Him all the prophets bear witness that through His name everyone who believes in Him receives forgiveness of sins."

REFLECT

Look at the places you marked *Jesus*. What did Peter preach about Him?

What did you learn from marking *peace*?

From verse 43 what did you learn about *everyone who believes*?

INSIGHT

Peace speaks of *completeness* and also of *harmonious relationships*; it is *a binding together of what has been at enmity, a joining of that which has been separated.*

When man rebelled against God's rule in the garden of Eden, he severed his intimate, loving relationship with God. Preferring to be his own master, he became an enemy of God. Jesus' death on man's behalf paid the full penalty for sin and removed guilt and condemnation. This made restoration to God's favor possible for those who believe. Through the blood of His cross, Jesus Christ satisfied the justice of God and reconciled all things to God, making peace (Colossians 1:20). He is God's only provision to bring man back into a right relationship with God. There is no other way to peace with God.

OBSERVE

We have seen what God did to provide salvation, but how does man need to respond? What must *we* do to be saved? What must *we* do to have peace with God?

Read Mark 1:14b-15; Luke 13:3, 5; and Acts 17:30-31:

- Mark *Jesus* (including pronouns and synonyms) with a cross. †
- Circle *gospel*.
- Mark *repent* with an arrow like this: ⟶

Mark 1:14b-15

14b ...Jesus came into Galilee, preaching the gospel of God,

15 and saying, "The time is fulfilled, and the kingdom of God is at hand; repent and believe in the gospel."

Luke 13:3, 5

3 "I [Jesus] tell you, no, but unless you repent, you will all likewise perish."

5 "I tell you, no, but unless you repent, you will all likewise perish."

Acts 17:30-31

30 "Therefore having overlooked the times of ignorance, God is now declaring to men that all *people* everywhere should repent,

31 because He has fixed a day in which He will judge the world in righteousness through a Man [Jesus Christ] whom He has appointed, having furnished proof to all men by raising Him from the dead."

REFLECT

What message did Jesus preach?

INSIGHT

The Greek word for **repent** means *to change one's mind—a complete change of attitude and thought concerning sin and righteousness.*

Repentance is a change of mind and heart which when genuine always results in a change of behavior. When we repent, we change our minds about God and His Son, Jesus, and acknowledge He is our Creator and Sovereign Ruler. We turn from a life of sin, which is living our lives independently from God: saying what **we** want to say, thinking what **we** want to think, going where **we** want to go, and doing what **we** want to do without regard to God and His Word; in short, being our own god. When we repent, we agree with what God says about sin and willingly *confess* it to Him and turn from it to God. We come under God's rightful and loving authority and live as He originally created us to live—in relationship with Him. When we receive His Spirit, we receive His Life. If we will not repent, we will perish.

How important is repentance?

OBSERVE

We have examined the first essential response to God's offer of salvation, repentance. Before we finish let's look at three more Scriptures.

Read Romans 2:4, Acts 11:18, and 2 Timothy 2:24-26 and mark:

- *God* with a triangle (including pronouns). △

- *repentance* with an arrow like this: ⟶⤵

Romans 2:4

4 Or do you think lightly of the riches of His kindness and tolerance and patience, not knowing that the kindness of God leads you to repentance?

Acts 11:18

18 When they heard this, they quieted down and glorified God, saying, "Well then, God has granted to the Gentiles also the repentance *that leads* to life."

2 Timothy 2:24-26

24 The Lord's bond-servant must not be quarrelsome, but be kind to all, able to teach, patient when wronged,

25 with gentleness correcting those who are in opposition, if perhaps God may grant them repentance leading to the knowledge of the truth,

26 and they may come to their senses *and escape* from the snare of the devil, having been held captive by him to do his will.

REFLECT

What did you learn from marking *God* and *repentance*?

Who grants repentance?

According to 2 Timothy 2:25-26, what happens when you repent?

Repentance

As we have learned this week, Jesus repeatedly said, "...unless you repent, you will all likewise perish" (Luke 13:3b and 5b). Often in today's presentation of the Gospel, people are asked to pray a sinner's prayer. The pastor, Bible teacher, or friend then recites a prayer to repeat. More often than not this prayer inadequately addresses repentance or doesn't at all. As a result, one can pray that prayer with a sincere heart and never come to the place of repentance or salvation. For this reason, we want to revisit repentance one more time from a biblical perspective.

What Repentance Is Not and What It Is

Repentance is not merely turning from wrong living and wrong actions. It is not a self-effort to clean up your life with a right mindset and strong will.

Repentance is not simply resolving to improve your behavior or attempting to live according to what is right. It is not just turning away from lying, cheating, being immoral, or being involved in sinful behaviors. It also is not a feeling of regret or worldly sorrow (2 Corinthians 7:8-11) for what you have done. It is not bargaining with God: "I'll stop this, if You do that."

Repentance is a radical, God-initiated change of perspective and direction of life, a turning from darkness to light, a deliberate yielding and submission to the LORD. It is motivated by a revelation of the LORD from the Word of God.

Recognizing His love toward you and your unworthiness, you surrender to Him, who alone gives new life and the ability to turn fully to Him.

Repentance occurs when:

- you come to a God-given awareness and authentic conviction of sin, realizing that nothing is hidden from God. You see your own sin as God sees it, confess it to Him, and renounce it. You realize that your sin has estranged you from your Creator and separated you from Him. You understand that you are without excuse because of who you are and what you have done.

- God imparts the realization that you must trust Him rather than yourself. Confronted by your self-centeredness, you no longer want to do what *seems* right in your own eyes but rather what *is* right in His eyes.

- God moves you to no longer live independently of Him but rather to live in conscious dependence upon Him. You entrust yourself to His rightful rule and authority over you as your Creator, and you seek to live in obedience to His commands in a personal, living relationship with Him.

- God gives you a longing for His promise to make you into a new person with a new heart and a new nature, and you understand your need to be changed at the very center of your being.

- God enables you to sense your need of transformation in your attitudes and morals, and you know that you are unable to generate this yourself. You turn to God, knowing that only He can do what you are unable to do yourself.

- believing God, you cease from your own efforts to save yourself, and you rest in Christ's completed work. The ideal motive for repentance is the desire to have fellowship with the holy and living God on His terms—not just to be forgiven and to find peace.

Regardless of whether you have lived a life of rebellion against God, living contrary to His Word and only for yourself or whether you have lived a life endeavoring to do good and to do what is right towards others—you must repent! Remember, Jesus says to all men everywhere, "...unless you repent, you will all likewise perish" (Luke 13:3b).

Without repentance you cannot find rest, salvation, and peace with God. They are by-products of a new life given by God in response to repentance and faith.

From the onset of our initial turning to God, we will probably never fully understand the depth of true repentance, but as we walk with Him and grow in our relationship with Jesus, He will give us greater understanding, drawing us ever deeper unto Himself.

Is God calling you to repent?

God's offer of salvation is a matter of life or death. Jesus taught more about hell, the destination for those who perish, than all the writers of the Scriptures. In several parables Jesus spoke of the wicked (the unrepentant sinner) being taken away from the righteous and cast into outer darkness and a fiery furnace where there is weeping and gnashing of teeth (see Matthew 13:49-50; 24:50-51; and 25:30).

What happens to those who do not repent, who choose to live their lives independently from God? Eternal death. This is not ceasing to exist but separation from God's personal presence and living forever in a place of great torment.

The Heart of The Matter

This week we examined Scriptures that define and explain the Gospel. We learned that the Gospel is all about Jesus Christ, the Promised One:

- Christ died for our sins according to the Scriptures.

- He was buried (evidence of His death).

- He was raised on the third day according to the Scriptures.

- After His resurrection, He appeared to Cephas (Peter), then to His twelve apostles, then to more than 500, then to James, then to all the apostles, then to Paul (1 Corinthians 15:4-8). Jesus proved His resurrection to these eyewitnesses who had watched His death. "To these He also presented Himself alive after His suffering, by many convincing proofs, appearing to them over *a period of* forty days and speaking of the things concerning the kingdom of God" (Acts 1:3).

Jesus preached, "The time is fulfilled, and the kingdom of God is at hand; repent and believe in the gospel" (Mark 1:15).

This week we learned that **repent** means *to change one's mind—a complete change of attitude and thought concerning sin and righteousness.* Repentance produces a change in behavior. Believers no longer desire to live independently from God, continuing to think and act contrary to His will.

In Christ, God grants repentance unto life, empowering men to come out from under the devil's authority and to come under God's rightful authority and His purpose for their lives. The initiative is God's. He reconciles all things; we have nothing to contribute. Only then do we have peace with God.

How do these truths about repentance apply to your life?

Week Eleven—*Believing the Gospel*

Last week we saw that God's plan to bring us into a right relationship with Him is centered in His Son, the Lord Jesus Christ. Sinners are rebels under the judgment and wrath of God. Choosing to go against God's way, living lives apart from Him; we are alienated from Him and on our way to destruction and eternal death. We desperately need a Savior.

The Gospel (*good news*) is that God has provided a way back to Himself through His Son who died in our place, paying the penalty for man's sin. Jesus was buried and descended into hell (*hades*), but death did not have the power to hold Him because Jesus was the sinless Lamb of God. On the third day, He was resurrected from the dead, proving that God, His Father, accepted His blood sacrifice for mankind's sin. The just requirements of God's Law had been satisfied.

Jesus said, "**Repent** and **believe** in the gospel" (Mark 1:15). In the last lesson we examined what it means to repent. This week we will learn what it means to believe the Gospel and what the Bible says about salvation.

OBSERVE

What does "believe the Gospel" mean?

Read John 20:30-31, Acts 16:30-31, and John 10:9:

- Underline *believe* and *believing*.
- Mark *Jesus* (including pronouns and titles) with a cross. †
- Mark *saved* with an arrow that goes under the word and then up like this: saved

John 20:30-31

30 Therefore many other signs Jesus also performed in the presence of the disciples, which are not written in this book;

31 but these have been written so that you may believe that Jesus is the Christ, the Son of God; and that believing you may have life in His name.

Acts 16:30-31

30 and after he brought them out, he said, "Sirs, what must I do to be saved?"

31 They said, "Believe in the Lord Jesus, and you will be saved, you and your household."

John 10:9

9 "I [Jesus] am the door; if anyone enters through Me, he will be saved, and will go in and out and find pasture."

REFLECT

What did you learn from marking *believe* and *believing*?

> ### INSIGHT
>
> The Greek word for the verb *believe* means *to be persuaded of, to place confidence in, to trust.* The noun *belief* or *faith* means *firm persuasion, conviction.*
>
> True biblical faith involves a firm conviction in the Gospel: who Jesus Christ is and the salvation He has accomplished for those who believe in Him. It also involves a personal surrender to Jesus Christ with an accompanying changed way of life reflected in one's thoughts, attitudes, words, and deeds that increasingly demonstrate a growing conviction and deepening surrender.

What did you learn from marking *saved*?

OBSERVE

Let's look at an important passage in John 3 where Jesus is answering a question from Nicodemus, a ruler of the Jews.

Read John 3:14-20:

- Mark *Jesus, Son,* and *Light* (including titles and pronouns) with a cross. †

- Underline *believe, believes,* and *believed.*

John 3:14-20

14 "As Moses lifted up the serpent in the wilderness, even so must the Son of Man [Jesus] be lifted up;

15 so that whoever believes will in Him have eternal life.

16 "For God so loved the world, that He gave His only begotten Son, that whoever believes in Him shall not perish, but have eternal life.

17 "For God did not send the Son into the world to judge the world, but that the world might be saved through Him.

18 "He who believes in Him is not judged; he who does not believe has been judged already, because he has not believed in the name of the only begotten Son of God.

19 "This is the judgment, that the Light has come into the world, and men loved the darkness rather than the Light, for their deeds were evil.

20 "For everyone who does evil hates the Light, and does not come to the Light for fear that his deeds will be exposed."

REFLECT

What did you learn from marking the references to *Jesus*? How is He described? What does He prophesy concerning Himself?

What did you learn from marking *believe*?

According to verses 16 and 17, why did God send Jesus into the world?

BACKGROUND

To understand what Jesus is saying in John 3:14 about being "lifted up," we must turn to the Old Testament.

Numbers 21 is a historical account of the LORD God judging His people by sending fiery serpents (poisonous snakes) among them because they were impatient and speaking against Him and Moses, His prophet. Many died from being bitten; so the people came to Moses confessing their sin and asking him to pray to the LORD for them, which he did.

The LORD did not remove the fiery serpents but commanded Moses to make a fiery serpent of brass and raise it up on a pole. People who were bitten were instructed to look at this serpent lifted up on the pole in order to live. Recognizing that they had the sentence of death upon them, they were to take God at His Word and look to the raised serpent to be healed. Thus God provided a way of salvation. It was not the people's faith, but God in whom they placed their faith, who was the source of their salvation. God used this event as a picture or type of what His Son would do for the people with regard to their sin.

Jesus was lifted up on the cross and crucified so that those who realize they have the sentence of death upon them can look to Him, believing that He has paid the debt for their sin with His blood. They are then saved. Like the bronze serpent, the cross is a symbol of the sentence of death, which Jesus suffered on our behalf. Now we look to Jesus Christ lifted up on the cross as God's provision for the forgiveness of our sins and for our salvation.

OBSERVE

Read Romans 10:9-11:

- Circle *confess* and *confesses*.
- Underline ***believe*** and ***believes***.

Romans 10:9-11

9 that if you confess with your mouth Jesus *as* Lord, and believe in your heart that God raised Him from the dead, you will be saved;

10 for with the heart a person believes, resulting in righteousness, and with the mouth he confesses, resulting in salvation.

11 For the Scripture says, "WHOEVER BELIEVES IN HIM WILL NOT BE DISAPPOINTED" [Isaiah 28:16].

REFLECT

What did you learn from marking *confess*?

INSIGHT
The Greek word translated ***confess*** means *to say the same thing, to declare, to make an emphatic declaration, to profess allegiance.*

What did you learn from marking *believe*?

OBSERVE

Read 2 Corinthians 4:3-4:

- Underline ***unbelieving*** (including pronouns) and put a backslash through the word like this: \

2 Corinthians 4:3-4

3 And even if our gospel is veiled, it is veiled to those who are perishing,

4 in whose case the god of this world has blinded the minds of the unbelieving so that they might not see the light of the gospel of the glory of Christ, who is the image of God.

REFLECT

What did you learn about the unbelieving?

From what you have learned about what it means to believe, have you *believed* on the Lord Jesus Christ?

INSIGHT
Faith is taking God at His Word. Therefore whatever the Bible says, we believe, agreeing with what He has declared and submitting to Him with a trusting, obedient heart.
Faith is not wanting something and then trying to believe God for it. This is a common but false concept of faith. Biblical faith has its origin and confidence in God, not in man's desires or perceived needs. It comes by hearing what God says, submitting to Him, and trusting Him to fulfill His promises as we make ourselves available to Him.
Romans 10:17 states, "So faith *comes* from hearing, and hearing by the word of Christ."

OBSERVE

Those who repent of their sin and believe the Gospel are "saved" from sin and condemnation; they are "born again," "Christians." Where do these terms come from?

Read John 3:1-8; Acts 11:25-26 and 26:27-29; and 1 Peter 4:15-17 and mark:

- *born again* and *born of the Spirit* with an upward arrow.
- *Christian* with an upward arrow.

John 3:1-8

1 Now there was a man of the Pharisees, named Nicodemus, a ruler of the Jews;

2 this man came to Jesus by night and said to Him, "Rabbi, we know that You have come from God *as* a teacher; for no one can do these signs that You do unless God is with him."

3 Jesus answered and said to him, "Truly, truly, I say to you, unless one is born again he cannot see the kingdom of God."

4 Nicodemus said to Him, "How can a man be born when he is old? He cannot enter a second time into his mother's womb and be born, can he?"

5 Jesus answered, "Truly, truly, I say to you, unless one is born of water and the Spirit he cannot enter into the kingdom of God.

6 "That which is born of the flesh is flesh, and that which is born of the Spirit is spirit.

7 "Do not be amazed that I said to you, 'You must be born again.'

8 "The wind blows where it wishes and you hear the sound of it, but do not know where it comes from and where it is going; so is everyone who is born of the Spirit."

Acts 11:25-26

25 And he [Barnabas] left for Tarsus to look for Saul;
26 and when he had found him, he brought him to Antioch. And for an entire year they met with the church and taught considerable numbers; and the disciples were first called Christians in Antioch.

Acts 26:27-29

27 "King Agrippa, do you believe the Prophets? I know that you do."
28 Agrippa *replied* to Paul, "In a short time you will persuade me to become a Christian."
29 And Paul *said*, "I would wish to God, that whether in a short or long time, not only you, but also all who hear me this day, might become such as I am, except for these chains."

1 Peter 4:15-17

15 Make sure that none of you suffers as a murderer, or thief, or evildoer, or a troublesome meddler;
16 but if *anyone suffers* as a Christian, he is not to be ashamed, but is to glorify God in this name.
17 For *it is* time for judgment to begin with the household of God; and if *it begins* with us first, what *will be* the outcome for those who do not obey the gospel of God?

REFLECT

What did you learn from marking *born again*? How important is it?

What did you learn from marking *Christian*?

The unbelieving, those separated from God by sin and unbelief, are spiritually dead. Are you born again? Are you a Christian?

OBSERVE

There are several misconceptions about how a person can be saved, find peace with God, and go to heaven. We will examine three of them in the light of Scripture.

The first misconception: Everyone who does good works will go to heaven.

What part do "works" or "good deeds" play in salvation?

Read Titus 3:4-8 and Ephesians 2:8-10:

- Mark *saved* with an arrow that goes under the word and then up like this: saved
- Underline *faith*.
- Mark *deeds* and *works* with a **W** (including pronouns).

Titus 3:4-8

4 But when the kindness of God our Savior and *His* love for mankind appeared,

5 He saved us, not on the basis of deeds which we have done in righteousness, but according to His mercy, by the washing of regeneration and renewing by the Holy Spirit,

6 whom He poured out upon us richly through Jesus Christ our Savior,

7 so that being justified by His grace we would be made heirs according to *the* hope of eternal life.

8 This is a trustworthy statement; and concerning these things I want you to speak confidently, so that those who have believed God will be careful to engage in good deeds. These things are good and profitable for men.

Ephesians 2:8-10

8 For by grace you have been saved through faith; and that not of yourselves, *it is* the gift of God;

9 not as a result of works, so that no one may boast.

10 For we are His workmanship, created in Christ Jesus for good works, which God prepared beforehand so that we would walk in them.

REFLECT

What did you learn from marking the word *saved*?

What did you learn from marking *works* or *deeds*?

Do our works or deeds save us? Explain.

Do "good works" come *before* our salvation or do they follow, confirming our salvation? Explain.

OBSERVE

The second misconception: Good people go to heaven.

It is often said in today's world, "Good people will go to heaven." What does God's Word say about this?

Read Luke 18:18-19 and Romans 3:10-12:

- Mark *good* with a check or tick ✓ over the word.

- Mark *none, no one* and *not even one* with an **X** through the word or words.

Luke 18:18-19

18 A ruler questioned Him, saying, "Good Teacher, what shall I do to inherit eternal life?"

19 And Jesus said to him, "Why do you call Me good? No one is good except God alone."

Romans 3:10-12

10 as it is written [Psalm 53:1-3],
> "THERE IS NONE RIGHTEOUS, NOT EVEN ONE;

11   THERE IS NONE WHO UNDERSTANDS,
THERE IS NONE WHO SEEKS FOR GOD;

12   ALL HAVE TURNED ASIDE, TOGETHER THEY HAVE
BECOME USELESS;
THERE IS NONE WHO DOES GOOD,
THERE IS NOT EVEN ONE."

REFLECT

What did you learn from marking *good*?

What did you learn from marking *none, no one, not even one*?

According to God's Word, can anyone be good enough to earn eternal life? Explain.

OBSERVE

The third misconception: There are many ways to God.

Have you ever said or heard others say that there are many ways to God? What does the Bible say? Is there any other way to be saved other than through Jesus Christ?

Read John 14:6, 1 Timothy 2:5, 6a, and Acts 4:12:

- Mark *Christ* and *Jesus* (including pronouns) with a cross. †

John 14:6

> 6 Jesus said to him, "I am the way, and the truth, and the life; no one comes to the Father but through Me."

1 Timothy 2:5, 6a

> 5 For there is one God, *and* one mediator also between God and men, *the* man Christ Jesus,
> 6a who gave Himself as a ransom for all, ...

Acts 4:12 (speaking of Jesus Christ)

> 12 "And there is salvation in no one else; for there is no other name under heaven that has been given among men by which we must be saved."

REFLECT

What did you learn about Jesus from these verses?

According to these Scriptures, are there many ways to God? Explain.

Remember, in Week Seven we saw Jesus in the garden of Gethsemane the night before His death. Jesus had lived His entire earthly life to please God, His Father. He had obeyed His Father in all things. Now, the night before He was to be mocked, beaten ("marred more than any man" [Isaiah 52:14]), crucified, and have the sins of man laid on Him, Jesus prayed, "...My Father, if it is possible, let this cup pass from Me; yet not as I will, but as You will" (Matthew 26:39b). Aware of the agony and suffering that lay ahead, Jesus prayed a second time, "...My Father, if this cannot pass away unless I drink it, Your will be done" (Matthew 26:42b). A third time, Jesus prayed, "...saying the same thing once more" (Matthew 26:44b).

In light of their relationship, how did God the Father respond to His Son's repeated request that night in Gethsemane?

The Father's response confirmed the reality that there was only one way for man to be saved and brought back into a right relationship with Him. That way was through the substitutionary blood sacrifice of a perfect, blameless, and sinless man. Jesus submitted Himself to the way of the cross. He did this willingly, "...becoming obedient to the point of death, even death on a cross" (Philippians 2:8b). "For indeed, the Son of Man is going as it has been determined;" (Luke 22:22a).

The Heart of The Matter

Let's summarize what we have learned over the last eleven weeks. There is no substitute for ongoing review and personal application.

From the very beginning the LORD God wanted to have a loving relationship and intimate fellowship with man whom He created to glorify Him and bring Him pleasure. Because of man's disobedience, sin entered the world and death followed. Thus through his choices, man entered into a hopeless state under the judgment of the LORD God. Instead of having peace with God, he became God's enemy, eternally alienated from the life and holiness of God's presence.

But because God so loved the world, He sent His only begotten Son, born of a virgin, into this world to become a man. As a man, Jesus lived a perfect and sinless life in total dependence upon His Father. He did nothing of His own initiative but only what He saw His Father doing (John 5:19, 30). The Holy Spirit fully indwelt Jesus and came upon Him at His baptism, anointing Him to do the works of God: teaching and preaching, signs, wonders, miracles, healing, and casting out demons.

He came in peace to bring us peace, but Jesus was persecuted, beaten, and crucified according to God's foreordained plan. He voluntarily submitted Himself to the cross, laying down His life for us. He shed His precious blood, paying the debt for our sins as our substitute, dying in our place. His body was buried. On the third day Jesus rose from the dead, fulfilling the Scriptures. God raised Jesus bodily from the dead to show that His sacrifice for us was accepted. Jesus then appeared to many people (over 500).

This is the Gospel, the good news! How will you respond?

Will you continue to go your own way believing that there are many ways to God, believing that doing your best will bring you God's peace and acceptance? This path leads to everlasting death. Or will you repent and believe the Gospel, receiving God's free gift of salvation through Jesus Christ? This is the only way to peace with God and to everlasting life.

Jesus said, "I am the resurrection and the life; he who believes in Me will live even if he dies, and everyone who lives and believes in Me will never die. Do you believe this?" (John 11:25-26).

Are you born again? Are you a Christian? Do you see sin as God sees it? Do you recognize His unselfish love for you and long to be transformed by Him? "Test yourselves *to see* if you are in the faith; examine yourselves! Or do you not recognize this about yourselves, that Jesus Christ is in you—unless indeed you fail the test [the Holy Spirit's witness to you that Christ is in you]?" (2 Corinthians 13:5).

Have you **repented** of your sin: a life of independence from God, rejecting His gracious and rightful rule over your life?

If you have not repented, then turn from your rebellion and indifference and submit to Him and to His rule over your life. Acknowledge that He is Lord and bow your knees to Him. What, if anything, is holding you back?

Have you ever truly **believed** in the Lord Jesus Christ—who He is and what He has done for you by dying in your place, shedding His blood, paying the ultimate price to reconcile you to God? If not, acknowledge that Jesus Christ is the Messiah, the Son of God, and the only way back to a right relationship and peace with God. Don't delay!

A person who has truly repented of his sin and has believed in Christ's death on his behalf as the only way to God has become a Christian. Christians are those who are trusting in God's Word; they recognize and confess that they have sinned against God and rightfully deserve the penalty of death. Acknowledging this, they daily repent and admit they are powerless to save themselves and are in need of a Savior. They believe in the death, burial, and resurrection of the Lord Jesus Christ and that He paid the full penalty for their sin. They believe He has removed their guilt and condemnation, satisfied God's justice, and they are now enabled to have peace and fellowship with Him. They believe that Christ's death on their behalf is the only way to God, and they live daily dependent upon Him as followers of Christ Jesus.

Ask yourself, "Have I come into this right relationship with God through His Son, and do I have peace with God?"

God hears the sincere prayer of the repentant heart that is prayed in the name of His Son, the Lord Jesus Christ. He longs for you to be in a right relationship with Him.

Week Twelve—*Walking in Newness of Life*

In our weeks together, we have been examining Scriptures that have shown us the Gospel, the *good news,* which is the power of God unto salvation. The Gospel has power to change rebellious hearts, power to free from sin, power to forgive and transform lives, and power to bring true inner peace.

This final week we will look at Scriptures that show what happens to us spiritually when we repent and turn to God in true faith. We will also observe how to live in light of so great a salvation.

This lesson is a long one, intended to firmly establish you in the faith. If you are constrained by time, feel free to divide it into two weeks.

OBSERVE

What happens when we're saved, when we're brought into a right relationship with God?

Read John 1:12-13, Colossians 1:12-14, and Romans 5:1:

- Mark **Lord Jesus Christ** and **Son** (including pronouns) with a cross. ✝

- Circle **children of God** and **saints** (including pronouns). ⬭

- Mark **peace** with a cloud.

John 1:12-13

12 But as many as received Him [Jesus Christ], to them He gave the right to become children of God, *even* to those who believe in His name,

13 who were born, not of blood nor of the will of the flesh nor of the will of man, but of God.

Colossians 1:12-14

12 giving thanks to the Father, who has qualified us to share in the inheritance of the saints in Light.

13 For He rescued us from the domain of darkness, and transferred us to the kingdom of His beloved Son,

14 in whom we have redemption, the forgiveness of sins.

Romans 5:1

1 Therefore, having been justified by faith, we have peace with God through our Lord Jesus Christ,

REFLECT

What happens to a person who receives Christ?

Where can you find peace with God?

OBSERVE

How does faith change a person's relationship with God?

Read Ephesians 2:13-14a, John 16:33, and Romans 8:16-17a:

- Mark *Christ Jesus* (including pronouns) with a cross. †
- Circle *children of God* and *heirs* (including pronouns).
- Mark *peace* with a cloud.

Ephesians 2:13-14a

13 But now in Christ Jesus you who formerly were far off have been brought near by the blood of Christ.

14a For He Himself is our peace,…

John 16:33

33 "These things I [Jesus Christ] have spoken to you, so that in Me you may have peace. In the world you have tribulation, but take courage; I have overcome the world."

Romans 8:16-17a

16 The Spirit Himself testifies [bears witness] with our spirit that we are children of God,

17a and if children, heirs also, heirs of God and fellow heirs with Christ…

REFLECT

What is the source of peace with God?

Does the Spirit of God bear witness with your spirit, confirming that you are a child of God?

OBSERVE

The Bible speaks of the Father, Son, and Holy Spirit each having a part in our salvation (1 Peter 1:2). What role does the Holy Spirit have in our salvation?

Read Ephesians 1:13-14a; Romans 8:9, 11, 14; and John 14:16-17, 19-20, and 26-27:

- Draw a cloud around *Holy Spirit, Spirit of truth,* and *Helper* (including all titles and pronouns).

Ephesians 1:13-14a

13 In Him [Christ], you also, after listening to the message of truth, the gospel of your salvation—having also believed, you were sealed in Him with the Holy Spirit of promise,

14a who is given as a pledge of our inheritance,...

Romans 8:9, 11, 14

9 However, you are not in the flesh but in the Spirit, if indeed the Spirit of God dwells in you. But if anyone does not have the Spirit of Christ, he does not belong to Him.

11 But if the Spirit of Him [God] who raised Jesus from the dead dwells in you, He who raised Christ Jesus from the dead will also give life to your mortal bodies through His Spirit who dwells in you.

14 For all who are being led by the Spirit of God, these are sons of God.

John 14:16-17, 19-20, 26-27

16 "I [Jesus] will ask the Father, and He will give you another Helper, that He may be with you forever;

17 *that is* the Spirit of truth, whom the world cannot receive, because it does not see Him or know Him, *but* you know Him because He abides with you and will be in you."

19 "After a little while the world will no longer see Me [Jesus], but you *will* see Me; because I live, you will live also.

20 "In that day you will know that I am in My Father, and you in Me, and I in you."

26 "But the Helper, the Holy Spirit, whom the Father will send in My name, He will teach you all things, and bring to your remembrance all that I said to you.

27 "Peace I leave with you; My peace I give to you; not as the world gives do I give to you. Do not let your heart be troubled, nor let it be fearful."

REFLECT

What did you learn by marking the *Holy Spirit*?

According to Jesus, what will the believer's relationship to the Holy Spirit be?

INSIGHT

The Holy Spirit is not an impersonal power or influence. Together with the Father and the Son, He lives, searches, teaches, witnesses, speaks, and guides.

The Spirit of God also sanctifies us (sets us apart) to God (2 Thessalonians 2:13 and 1 Peter 1:2). He separates us from the world, from the life that rejects the rule of God.

In John 16 we learn that the Spirit "...will convict the world concerning sin and righteousness and judgment;" (vs. 8b). The Spirit will guide us into all truth. "...He will not speak on His own initiative, but whatever He hears, He will speak; and He will disclose to you what is to come. He will glorify Me [Jesus Christ],..." (vs. 13b-14a).

OBSERVE

Just as we cannot save ourselves by our own efforts, once we receive Christ we cannot live our new life by our own efforts. We do not just turn over a new leaf. We cannot become better, more moral persons by our own determination and exertion alone. On the contrary, having received the life of Christ, we now trust Him to do His work in us by the Holy Spirit.

Who is the source of our new life?

Read 2 Corinthians 5:17; 1 John 5:11-12, 20; and John 20:30-31:

- Mark *Jesus, Christ,* and *Son* (including pronouns) with a cross. ✝
- Circle *life*.

2 Corinthians 5:17

17 Therefore if anyone is in Christ, *he is* a new creature; the old things passed away; behold, new things have come.

1 John 5:11-12, 20

11 And the testimony is this, that God has given us eternal life, and this life is in His Son.
12 He who has the Son has the life; he who does not have the Son of God does not have the life.

20 And we know that the Son of God has come, and has given us understanding so that we may know Him who is true; and we are in Him who is true, in His Son Jesus Christ. This is the true God and eternal life.

John 20:30-31

30 Therefore many other signs Jesus also performed in the presence of the disciples, which are not written in this book;
31 but these have been written so that you may believe that Jesus is the Christ, the Son of God; and that believing you may have life in His name.

REFLECT

What did you learn from marking *Christ*?

What did you learn from marking *life*?

When does eternal life begin for a believer? Why?

INSIGHT

In John 20:30-31, John states why he wrote his Gospel: so that readers might **believe** that Jesus is the Christ, the Son of God, and have **life** in His name.

OBSERVE

We do not come before God with our own merit but rely on the completed work of Christ on the cross. Jesus Christ is not only our Lord and Savior, but He is also our very life.

What can we learn from the following Scriptures that will give us more understanding?

Read Romans 5:10 and Romans 6:4:

- Mark *Son* and *Christ* (including pronouns) with a cross. †
- Circle *life*.

Romans 5:10

10 For if while we were enemies we were reconciled to God through the death of His Son, much more, having been reconciled, we shall be saved by His life.

Romans 6:4

4 Therefore we have been buried with Him through baptism into death, so that as Christ was raised from the dead through the glory of the Father, so we too might walk in newness of life.

REFLECT

What did you learn from marking *Son* and *Christ*?

What did you learn from marking *life*?

INSIGHT

As we studied last week, Christ died *for* us, taking on the penalty for sin we deserved. When we repent and believe, the Father sees us "**in Him**." Romans 6 states that when Jesus died, we died with Him. A permanent and decisive break from the penalty and power of sin was made. When He was buried, we were buried with Him. When Jesus was raised from the dead, we were raised with Him to walk in newness of life. We have new life (His life) in union with Him.

OBSERVE

How are we enabled to live as Christians and empowered to walk in newness of life?

Read Ezekiel 36:26-27, Jeremiah 31:33b, and Jeremiah 32:39-40 and mark:

- *God* (including pronouns) with a triangle. △

- *covenant* with a slash. /

Ezekiel 36:26-27

26 "Moreover, I [God] will give you a new heart and put a new spirit within you; and I will remove the heart of stone from your flesh and give you a heart of flesh.

27 "I will put My Spirit within you and cause you to walk in My statutes, and you will be careful to observe My ordinances."

Jeremiah 31:33b

33b "... I [God] will put My law within them and on their heart I will write it; and I will be their God, and they shall be My people."

Jeremiah 32:39-40

39 "and I [God] will give them one heart and one way, that they may fear Me always, for their own good and for *the good of* their children after them.

40 "I will make an everlasting covenant with them that I will not turn away from them, to do them good; and I will put the fear of Me in their hearts so that they will not turn away from Me."

REFLECT

These three passages describe the New Covenant God makes with all believers. What promises does He make to enable you to walk as a Christian?

OBSERVE

Although at times we falter, God wants us to no longer walk as unbelievers. Since God has made us new creatures in Christ, how has our walk (behavior, manner of life) changed?

What does "walk in newness of life" mean?

Read Colossians 1:10b, 2 Corinthians 5:7, and 1 John 2:6:

- Mark *Lord* (including pronouns) with a cross. †
- Underline *walk*.

Colossians 1:10b

10b...walk in a manner worthy of the Lord, to please *Him* in all respects, bearing fruit in every good work and increasing in the knowledge of God;

2 Corinthians 5:7

7 for we walk by faith, not by sight—

1 John 2:6

6 the one who says he abides in Him [Jesus Christ] ought himself to walk in the same manner as He walked.

REFLECT

According to these verses, how are we to *walk* (live)?

OBSERVE

If we are to walk as Jesus walked, how did He walk on earth?

Read John 5:19b, 30 and John 8:28-29:

- Mark **Son** and **Jesus** (including pronouns) with a cross. †

John 5:19b, 30

19b …"Truly, truly, I [Jesus Christ] say to you, the Son
can do nothing of Himself, unless *it is* something He
sees the Father doing; for whatever the Father does,
these things the Son also does in like manner."

30 "I [Jesus Christ] can do nothing on My own initiative.
As I hear, I judge; and My judgment is just, because
I do not seek My own will, but the will of Him [God
His Father] who sent Me."

John 8:28-29

28 So Jesus said, "When you lift up [crucify] the Son
of Man, then you will know that I am *He,* and I do
nothing on My own initiative, but I speak these
things as the Father taught Me.

29 "And He [the Father] who sent Me is with Me; He
has not left Me alone, for I always do the things that
are pleasing to Him."

REFLECT

How did Jesus live on earth? What was His relationship to His Father?

Are you walking as Jesus walked?

INSIGHT

It is vital to understand that when Jesus Christ walked on earth He lived in total dependence on God His Father for everything. He never initiated or did anything apart from His Father's leading. Fully God and fully man, He lived the perfect life God created man to live—completely dependent on God through the Spirit.

Even when Jesus Christ performed signs, wonders, miracles, and cast out demons, He never initiated these actions; He did them by the Spirit of God working through Him (Acts 10:38).

OBSERVE

How can we better understand what it means to be given a new heart, enabling us to walk in faith, to live dependent on God, and to walk as Jesus walked?

Let's look at an allegory in John 15 that Jesus spoke to His disciples.

Read John 15:1-5:

- Mark *I, Me,* and *vine* (including pronouns) with a cross. †
- Circle *branch* and *branches* (including pronouns).

John 15:1-5

1 "I [Jesus] am the true vine, and My Father is the vinedresser.

2 "Every branch in Me that does not bear fruit, He takes away; and every *branch* that bears fruit, He prunes it so that it may bear more fruit.

3 "You are already clean because of the word which I have spoken to you.

4 "Abide in Me, and I in you. As the branch cannot bear fruit of itself unless it abides in the vine, so neither *can* you, unless you abide in Me.

5 "I am the vine, you are the branches; he who abides in Me and I in him, he bears much fruit, for apart from Me you can do nothing."

REFLECT

What did you learn by marking references to *Jesus Christ*?

From what you learned from marking *branch*, what should characterize the believer's relationship with Jesus Christ?

Why is it important to stay connected to Christ?

INSIGHT

The Christian life is Christ living His life in and through us while we live in an attitude of total dependence on Him. By His Spirit He initiates, empowers, and does His will through us. As a result, we express His life, and He receives all the glory.

OBSERVE

The gift of salvation brings us back into a living, intimate relationship with God. Through His life and death, Jesus reconciled man to God so that we can live as He created us to live.

We no longer live for ourselves. The life of Christ within us enables us to glorify God—to reflect and give a correct testimony of who He is. We have a new desire to daily seek God and grow in our knowledge of Him. He does not want a half-hearted commitment. His living presence, prayer, and God's Word instruct and empower us to live a life that is pleasing to Him.

We are not left on our own. We become Christ-like as God's Spirit produces Christ's life within us. Christ-likeness is not our acting like or living for Christ *in our own strength*, nor is it doing what is "right in our own eyes" in His name. We are like Christ because He is living the essence of His life in and through us.

We read the Bible and cling to His promises. Our union with Him is a life of dependence on Him: seeking Him and His will in everything, a life led by His Spirit.

In Him we are no longer bound by sin, nor under its dominion, but we must daily choose to say "No" to temptations when they arise. When we choose to live our lives in obedience to His Word and to the promptings of His Spirit, Christ in us brings forth the life that is pleasing to God, glorifying Him in our thoughts, words, attitudes, and deeds.

Read Galatians 2:20 and 2 Corinthians 5:14-15:

- Mark **Christ** (including all titles and pronouns) with a cross. †

Galatians 2:20

20 "I have been crucified with Christ; and it is no longer
I who live, but Christ lives in me; and the *life* which
I now live in the flesh I live by faith in the Son of
God, who loved me and gave Himself up for me.

2 Corinthians 5:14-15

14 For the love of Christ controls us, having concluded
this, that one died for all, therefore all died;
15 and He died for all, so that they who live might no
longer live for themselves, but for Him who died and
rose again on their behalf.

REFLECT

What did you learn from these verses about Christ?

How should what Christ did on our behalf affect us and work out in our
daily lives?

The Heart of The Matter

This week we learned that when we repent of our sin and believe the Gospel:

- We are reconciled to God by the death of His Son.
- We are delivered from the power of darkness and transferred into the kingdom of the Son.
- We become a new creature in Christ with old things passing away and everything becoming new.
- We become children of God.
- We have forgiveness of sins through His blood.
- We are buried and raised with Christ so that we might walk in newness of life.
- We receive eternal life in God's Son.
- We are sealed in Christ with the Holy Spirit who is given to us as a pledge of our inheritance.
- The Spirit of God dwells within us and bears witness that we are children of God.
- The Spirit of truth teaches us.
- Jesus gives us Himself and His peace.
- Through the New Covenant in His blood He gives us all we need to live as new creatures in Him.
- We are saved by His life.

We now know that we must:

- walk in a manner worthy of the Lord.
- walk by faith and not by sight.
- walk as Jesus walked—in total dependence on God.
- abide in Christ, knowing that apart from Him we can do nothing.

As you read the previous page and worked through this study, perhaps you realized that you do not have a living relationship with Jesus Christ. You may have knowledge of the historical faith, involvement in a church, and religious sympathies; but *still* you do not have peace with God.

Is God's Spirit saying to you, "It is time to act on all that you have learned and all that you know about the Promised One, the Messiah Jesus Christ"? Take time to think about it. Your decision has eternal consequences. It truly is a life and death matter. Choose life!

Repent of your sin and receive forgiveness from God based on Christ's finished work on the cross. Believe the good news of the Gospel; believe Him to be your Savior, Lord, and your very Life. This is the **only** way to peace with God and everlasting life.

We were not created to live independently from God. As our Creator, He knows our ultimate well-being comes only from a right relationship with the risen Lord. Once you have committed your life to Him, God sees you *in* His Son, buried with Him and raised with Him. He calls you to walk in newness of life and empowers you to live a life pleasing to Him. As you read God's Word, pray, worship, and "trust and obey," His Spirit begins to conform you to His nature. He transforms you, changing you into His image. He gives you His peace. In a relationship with Him, you can love Him and know Him in a growing intimacy. This is an ongoing process. All you need for living a godly life you will find in Him (2 Peter 1:3).

God is willing and able to save and to give peace to all who come to Him—His way.

You can have peace with God!

Now may the God of hope fill you with all joy and peace in believing, so that you will abound in hope by the power of the Holy Spirit.
ROMANS 15:13

Be anxious for nothing, but in everything by prayer and supplication with thanksgiving let your requests be made known to God. And the peace of God, which surpasses all comprehension, will guard your hearts and minds in Christ Jesus.
PHILIPPIANS 4:6-7

Now may the God of peace Himself sanctify you entirely; and may your spirit and soul and body be preserved complete, without blame at the coming of our Lord Jesus Christ.
1 THESSALONIANS 5:23

Now the God of peace, who brought up from the dead the great Shepherd of the sheep through the blood of the eternal covenant, even *Jesus our Lord, equip you in every good thing to do His will, working in us that which is pleasing in His sight, through Jesus Christ, to whom* be *the glory forever and ever. Amen.*
HEBREWS 13:20-21

"Peace I leave with you; My peace I give to you;"
JOHN 14:27a

CPSIA information can be obtained at www.ICGtesting.com
Printed in the USA
LVOW05s0015041014

407199LV00008B/102/P